Books by Robert Ackart

A Celebration of
Vegetables

A CELEBRATION

DRAWINGS BY MARJORIE ZAUM

New York   1979   *Atheneum*

Robert Ackart

OF VEGETABLES

Menus for Festive Meat-Free Dining

Library of Congress Cataloging in Publication Data
Ackart, Robert C
  A celebration of vegetables.
  Includes index.
  1. Cookery (Vegetables)   I. Title.
TX801.A26   641.6'5   77–76469
ISBN 0–689–70581–6

Published simultaneously in Canada by
McClelland and Stewart Ltd.
Manufactured in the United States of America by
The Book Press, Brattleboro, Vermont
Designed by Kathleen Carey
First Atheneum Paperback Printing February 1979
Second Printing November 1979

For Ellen and Tage Fagergren

Introduction

This book is a celebration of vegetables. It is written about their joyous preparation and festive presentation. Vegetables can be *the* meal, not merely the accompaniment to other foods. They can be as exciting and tasty and every bit as delicious as main dishes of meat or fish. Vegetables are beautiful, flavorful, and can be creatively combined in innumerable ways to produce elegant meals.

There are many books on vegetable cookery, but very few, to my best knowledge, are concerned with vegetables for their own sake. Many view their subject as a kind of necessary adjunct to meats and fish; they begrudgingly give the nod to oven-browned potatoes and braised Brussels sprouts when the *real* focus is on the roast lamb. Some point out, in crusading tones, that vegetables *must* be eaten for the sake of good health, and they make the preparation and eating of vegetables a kind of therapy. And, particularly nowadays, because they are reasonably inexpensive—and thus kind to the household budget— vegetables are presented as second-best substitutes for meat.

It is true that vegetables are, for the most part, less expensive than meat. It is equally true that vegetables are "good for us." And, to augment an already established vegetarian philosophy, there is a growing trend toward more frequent meatless meals being stimulated by the feeling—shared by many thoughtful people—that a "meat diet" is *not* as healthy as we are asked to believe, that it wastes natural and national resources, and that it is neither economically nor morally defensible.

But, these considerations aside, vegetable cookery is pleasurable. Buying vegetables at the supermarket or greengrocer's is enjoyable, working with them in the kitchen is easy and creative, and serving them attractively at table provides us an elegant way of dining. This book offers a change from ordinary daily menu-making, a new and stimulating experience for the cook in the kitchen and for the diners at table.

I should say at the outset that this is not a vegetarian cookbook; I am not a vegetarian. I eat meats and enjoy them. I also eat vegetables and enjoy *them*. I find them as satisfying as chicken or beef or lamb, for example—indeed, they *can* be made tastier, for in their variety of flavors and textures, they far outdistance meats.

I am often asked, "Can one eat vegetables without gaining weight?" Yes: in organizing this book and experimenting with its recipes, I have happily enjoyed a vegetable diet, virtually meat-free. I have rid myself of several unwanted pounds and feel better for having done so. Butter on vegetables? Dishes made with olive oil? Yes, as much as I want of either, because in many instances vegetables contain fewer calories to begin with than does meat; with a lower calorie "base," butter, oil, or sauces may be added without exceeding the calories of a meat dish. The paramount consideration with vegetable meals—as, indeed, with all meals—is that they be properly balanced. These menus, I believe, fulfill that criterion. And it is also important that carbohydrates and farinaceous foods be eaten with thoughtful moderation; in Chapter VI the reader will find a few recipes for rice, bulgur and potatoes, as well as a limited selection of quick breads, to be used at the option of the cook and to add substance to the menus when desired. Many menus offer ways to prepare vegetables more plainly as simple alternatives to suggested dishes.

Writing this book has been a stimulating and creative experience. Nothing gives me greater pleasure than evolving a new dish or adapting and giving a different interest to a standard one. Cooking is gratifyingly inventive and rewarded by the companionship shared with others at table. My hope for readers using this book is that they, too, will adapt menus and recipes to their own tastes, adding their own personal touches. Therein lie the rewards of cooking and the *raison d'être* for any cookbook.

In these days of high food prices, however, the pleasures of vegetables may well begin not in your kitchen, but in your garden. The book offers some unusual ways to use your own produce and includes some uncommon vegetables which may be home grown and which are not always available at the supermarket; their use will give your menus added originality. Whether your foods are home-garnered or supermarket-purchased, effort is made here to follow the seasons: As spring and summer vegetables appear, they are used at their best and freshest; as the months pass, the menus utilize later produce until, in autumn and winter, meals are enhanced by vegetables appropriate to the waning year. Although the book suggests use of home-grown foods to lend added zest to a subject already filled with pleasures, most of us shop in supermarkets (if we are fortunate, we may also buy from an old-fashioned neighborhood greengrocer). Therefore, the book is designed primarily for homemakers across the nation who, perforce, buy at grocery stores and supermarkets, where variety may be limited. For this reason, recipes calling for "unusual" vegetables are accompanied by alternatives.

The menus are composed of fresh and, because of seasonal lack or for the sake of convenience, frozen vegetables. Only infrequently do I recommend use of canned vegetables which, while healthy enough, have neither the taste nor the color nor the texture of fresh or—if properly handled—frozen ones; in suggesting use of canned products, I hope to save the reader shopping difficulties and unnecessary time spent in the kitchen.

The menus suggest a first course, a main dish, complementary side dishes, a salad, if desirable, and a dessert. Some of the dishes, such as soups and desserts, are repeated in different menus. But with the exception of soufflés (used as first course for six persons and as main dish for four) and a few other recipes suitable as both appetizer and principal plate of the meal, few main dishes are used more than once. Both menus and recipes, adapted to a format which, I feel, is easily read and easily used, are designed to serve usually six, but sometimes four, persons. Many of the recipes may be either fully prepared or readied for cooking well ahead of time. Indication is made whenever this treatment is possible. The practice results, I must admit, from my being, perhaps, a lazy cook and, more importantly, a sociable one: I do not want many last minute things to do while family or friends are in the living room having cocktails. I want to enjoy the fun with them. These menus are designed to allow you to enjoy the fun, too.

It is my hope that the book will be attractive to people who want to extend their pleasure in cooking and dining through acquaintance with intriguing and festive vegetable meals.

Robert Ackart

KATONAH, NEW YORK
1977

Contents

A Celebration of

Vegetables

To Enjoy This Book More Fully

The following suggestions are made to facilitate and make pleasanter your time in the kitchen and to afford you a more attractive table when you serve family and friends.

First, a few general instructions on using the book:

The length of time required to prepare the dishes and the length of time required to cook them are stated at the start of each recipe. Preparation times are approximate, depending upon the expertise of the cook; the times given apply to cooks a bit better than average in efficiency, organization, and know-how . . . and include the actual peeling, chopping, and other preparation of vegetables used as ingredients in the recipe. It is assumed that, when possible, two or three steps in the preparation will be simultaneously undertaken. The cooking time given refers to that period required to finish the assembled dish or, in other words, to that cooking which must be done *following* the suggestion, *"At this point you may stop and continue later."* This latter direction is given to indicate recipes that may be made either in one session or, if preferred, in two; it is omitted when the recipe is really more easily or effectively prepared in a single period. If a recipe is oven-cooked, the temperature setting is given at the outset, so that the oven will be ready when the dish is to go into it. Ingredients are listed in the order of their use, and for cooks who, like myself, arrange their condiment shelves alphabetically, herbs and spices are listed that way.

BOUILLON CUBES ARE AN INGREDIENT . . .

frequently used in these recipes. I suggest using vegetable bouillon cubes, but you are not obliged to follow the suggestion. I have made these recipes with vegetable bouillon cubes and powder, chicken bouillon cubes and powder, and—best of all—with vegetable stock, homemade from peelings, stem ends, and so forth, replacing the liquid called for by the recipe.

3

BUTTER IS CALLED FOR IN THESE RECIPES . . .

but margarine works as a dependable substitute if you prefer to use it, and it *is* free of cholesterol, although it is no less fattening than butter.

You will find, I believe, that sweet or unsalted butter will improve these dishes; the delicate flavors of vegetables respond to sweet butter rather better than they do to salted. The suggested amounts of seasonings assume the use of sweet butter.

CHILLING IN THE FREEZER . . .

is a speedy but chancy way to finish a mousse or cold soufflé or any other dish that may require setting. If you attempt this method, stand close watch and at the *very* moment you detect even one hint of an ice crystal, move the dish to the refrigerator. As a lazy cook, I prefer to make the recipe sufficiently in advance of serving so that I know that six good hours remain in which the dish can do its thing without my being on hand to police it.

COOKWARE SHOULD BE ATTRACTIVE . . .

and it can be. You will note that often the suggestion to use an "oven-proof serving dish" is made—a time- and work-saving boon to the cook. Cook-and-serve ware is available in all shapes and sizes, all designs and colors, from attractive electric skillets to handsome enamelized iron utensils.

CREAM IS OFTEN CALLED FOR . . .

in these recipes. And cream undeniably makes many dishes more glamorous. But it is not always necessary to use cream if you are calorie- or cholesterol-conscious. Experimentation has shown that, on a scale of preference, one can use heavy cream (if called for) or light cream or "half-and-half" or homogenized milk. Evaporated milk may also be used in some dishes whose flavor is pronounced (in garlic soup, for example, or broccoli bisque, or in various desserts). Skimmed or nonfat dried milk, however, make a poor showing in these recipes. Using them as substitutes will affect the flavor and texture of the completed dish; the result is generally one of increased lightness.

IF YOU PREFER NOT TO MAKE DESSERT . . .

The desserts suggested in these menus can be made with little effort on your part. Sometimes, however, either time limitations or your own choice dictate a dessert different from the one offered; in these instances, do as I do: serve cheese and fresh fruit. Ideally, cheese is served as a course by itself so that its subtlety of flavor does not compete with other tastes. But there are times when cheese and fruit together produce a perfect marriage: sharp Cheddar and crisp apples, for example, or a piece of Parmesan served with a ripe pear (a combination I discovered many years ago in Italy and have served ever since). One suggestion: our greengrocers and supermarkets are shipped fruit picked before it is ripe; to make sure that the fruit of your choice will be served at its best, buy it a few days in advance, allow it to ripen, preferably at room temperature, and when it is ripe, store it for a day or two in the refrigerator.

ELECTRIC BLENDERS . . .

How did we ever cook without them? They are helpful in preparing these recipes because they combine flavors instantaneously and produce purées of absolute smoothness in about the same length of time. These days, I suppose, nearly every kitchen is equipped with an electric blender; but if you do not own one, do not be daunted. Write "electric blender" at the top of your birthday gift list and proceed happily to prepare with a food mill the recipes calling for its more sophisticated cousin. Do not overfill the container of an electric blender. The immediate impulse of the gadget, once turned on, is *upward*; too frequently I have found on the ceiling hints of the soup I was blending. For this reason, I suggest that you fill the container of the blender two cups at a time.

There are available food processors which do just about anything, from making sauces to chopping, from slicing to puréeing. I do not suggest their purchase, but, if you have one or are considering acquiring one, you will find that it does effectively all jobs which, in this book, are assigned to the more commonly used electric blender.

FREEZING . . .

vegetable dishes is risky, and I do not recommend it for these recipes, either cooked or uncooked, because of the high water content of their ingredients. When freezing is possible—as with soups, for example— notation to that effect is given.

A WORD OF SOLACE TO THE
HOME GARDENER . . .

It is unlikely that any private vegetable garden will provide at one and the same time all vegetables needed for menus directed to gardening amateurs. Wide variations of climate and the many different growing conditions throughout America indicate that only a few home-grown vegetables will be ready for any single menu. No matter, making your vegetable garden a part of this book, as surely I have made mine, is intended not as integral to the purpose of the book, but as an added enjoyment to the pleasures of vegetable dining.

THERE ARE REASONS FOR FREQUENT
USE OF JELLIED DISHES . . .

They may be made well ahead of time; their presentation, especially if unmolded in a pleasing form, is festive and elegant; and they are an excellent source of protein in meatless meals.

IF YOU WANT TO MAKE YOUR OWN MENU . . .

The suggested menus offer combinations of foods which I have enjoyed; these combinations are, therefore, highly personal. One aim of this book is to stimulate you to create *your* menus, too; and if you do so, I will feel the book has truly succeeded. To help you compose menus of your own, you will find at the front of the index all dishes listed alphabetically according to their menu categories (Appetizers, Soups, Main Dishes, Vegetable Side Dishes, and so forth).

A MICROWAVE OVEN . . .

If you have one (and they seem to be increasingly popular in private homes) is a helpful boon to vegetable cookery. I do not suggest that you purchase one for they are expensive appliances; but if you are already the happy owner of a microwave oven, you will find yourself a master vegetable cook in a surprisingly short time. Because it uses very little water, or sometimes none at all, in cooking raw vegetables, the microwave oven preserves to a remarkable degree the taste, color, texture, and nutritional value of vegetables.

MUSHROOMS . . .

may need your attention before you cook them. If they are beautiful, satin-white ones, you need only trim the very ends of their stems. If, however, they seem less than perfectly clean or are slightly spotted, rub the caps gently with a damp cloth or paper towel; you will find that they clean easily and quickly. Then trim the stem ends and proceed with the recipe as directed.

THERE ARE REASONS FOR FREQUENT USE OF THE OVEN . . .

My laziness and dislike of clutter—those are two reasons for my frequent use of the oven. There are others certainly more cogent: cooking in the oven allows the cook greater freedom; it provides a cleaner kitchen to work in; it obviates to great extent the possibility of scorching or burning the dish; and, in many instances, it assures that the meal will arrive at table on time, hot, and—if you use cook-and-serve utensils—attractively presented.

OVERCOOKING IS THE RUIN . . .

of vegetables and vegetable cookery. For the sake of the pleasures I hope you will derive from these recipes, do not spoil the taste, color, texture, and nutritional value of their ingredients by over-boiling, -baking, or -broiling them. When boiling vegetables, use as little water as possible or, if convenient, steam them to best retain their flavor and consistency. I have purposely stated cooking times that should yield tender-crisp vegetables. Remember that vegetables continue to cook after they have been removed from the range or oven; for this reason, I often suggest refreshing by running under or plunging into cold water partially cooked vegetables which are to be used as the ingredient of a particular recipe.

GRATED PARMESAN CHEESE . . .

in my kitchen always means *freshly* grated Parmesan cheese. Yes, there are available various brands of prepared grated Italian or Italian-type cheese, but they are at best only distant cousins of Italy's king of cheeses, the superb *Parmigiana*. In Italy this *grana* cheese, so called because of the hard and minute crystals which form part of its texture, is used as a table cheese *and* as a condiment in cooking. Its rich, salty-fresh flavor is volatile and cannot be imprisoned in a cardboard shaker. Buy a piece of Parmesan, preferably imported, and grate it as you need it (the cheese keeps very well when sealed tightly in plastic wrap and refrigerated).

SAVE AND USE VEGETABLE PEELINGS . . .

Whenever a recipe calls for peeling or scraping a rinsed vegetable, re-serve the peel, refrigerated. When you have a substantial quantity of mixed vegetable peelings, make bouillon, just as you would prepare chicken or meat stock from trimmings and table leavings. Season the stock with onion, garlic, bay leaf, rosemary perhaps, thyme, a little sugar, salt, and pepper. Sieve the stock, discarding the peelings, and store it in the refrigerator or freezer for use as the liquid ingredient in these recipes (desserts excepted) whenever water or bouillon is called for. So doing will enhance the flavor of the dishes and will add to their nutritional value without augmenting their calorie count.

REFRIGERATION . . .

of vegetable dishes is a tricky business. When it is possible to refrigerate a cooked recipe, notation to that effect is given. Most often, however, a prepared and assembled but *un*cooked recipe—especially if it is *en casserole*—may, if desired, be refrigerated. It is important that the ingredients then come fully to room temperature before cooking. Because of the high water content of vegetables, refrigeration will often destroy the texture of a completed dish.

THERE ARE REASONS FOR THE LIMITED NUMBER OF SALADS IN THE MENUS . . .

In a menu composed of vegetables, to serve salad with every meal seems, to me, not only a redundancy, but also an exaggeration. Salads, of all dishes, are perhaps the most "personal"; the best ones are products of the cook's flight of fancy. To stimulate that flight, suggestions for salads are given in Chapter VI.

IF YOU ARE DIRECTED TO SCALD MILK OR CREAM . . .

The old-fashioned way of scalding milk and cream called for bringing them briefly to the boil. Nonsense! Boiling changes their flavor and makes the pan very difficult to clean. Scald them the easy way: in the top of a double boiler over boiling water, heat the milk or cream until it shimmers and a thin film develops over its surface. That is all there is to it—and the top of the double boiler will wash clean without scrubbing.

SOUFFLES . . .

are easy to make, elegant to serve, and always appreciated. I have found that soufflés are successful if their ingredients are readied ahead of actual preparation and cooking. To make a successful, easily prepared soufflé, measure and ready *all* ingredients and have them at room temperature; butter the soufflé dish. Prepare the *roux* (combination of butter and flour as called for), then *stop and continue later*. The final preparation and mixing of soufflé ingredients are very rapid and should be done just at the point when the soufflé is to be cooked.

SOUP . . .

of the evening, beautiful soup! But why so many of them, compared to other first courses? (There are other first courses in this book, but the majority are soups because of the satisfactions I list here.) First, soups are all make-ahead dishes; no last minute frenzy with them. Second, they not only make ahead, they make ahead and freeze (you need only allow a frozen soup to thaw fully to room temperature before homogenizing it in the container of an electric blender, then heating or chilling it, as you prefer). The possibility of freezing soups explains why I suggest the use of scalded milk or cream in making them, for scalding reduces the chances of their separating or curdling. Third, the majority of soups in this book may be served either hot or cold; thus you may use a "winter" soup in summer, if you choose. Fourth, all soup recipes make six or more servings, a fact allowing you to freeze and later to combine leftover soups to make "new" ones of different flavors. Fifth, in the interests of simplifying kitchen work, I have restricted thickened soups to two kinds—flour- and potato-thickened; once these two simple techniques are mastered, you can easily make the greater number of soups in this book. Sixth, soup, hot or cold, following cocktails, is kind to the stomach, awakens appetite without satiating it, and prepares both digestion and spirit for the meal to follow.

The following vegetables are used in these menus:

Artichokes	Kale
Asparagus	Kohlrabi
Beans, green	Leeks
Beans, lima	Mushrooms
Beets	Okra
Broccoli	Onions
Brussels sprouts	Parsnips
Cabbage, green	Peas, green
Cabbage, red	Peas, snow
Carrots	Potatoes
Cauliflower	Peppers
Celery	Pumpkins
Celery root (celeriac)	Scallions (or green onions)
Chinese cabbage	Spinach
Corn	Squash, summer
Cucumber	Squash, winter
Eggplant	Swiss chard
Endive	Tomatoes
Fennel	Turnips
Jerusalem artichokes	

From them you can devise many recipes of your own. Or you can use the index of recipes, presented under their menu categories (appetizers, soups, main dishes, etc.), to assemble combinations of foods attractive to you, and thus create your own menus.

Menus for Spring

Cucumber and Spinach Soup
Scallion Quiche
Carrots Glazed in Honey
Green Peas with Mint
Apricot Pudding

FOR 6 PERSONS

A menu designed for home gardeners or for food shoppers who are particular and persevering because, ideally, these vegetables should be young and very fresh. You may make the soup and pudding a day before and refrigerate them.

Cucumber and Spinach Soup

DOUBLES / REFRIGERATES / FREEZES

PREPARATION: 45 MINUTES

Serve the soup hot or cold, garnished with a sprinkling of dill weed.

3 cups water
4 vegetable bouillon cubes
1 medium onion, peeled and chopped coarse
3 medium cucumbers, peeled and chopped coarse
One 10-ounce package fresh spinach, rinsed
1 medium potato, peeled and chopped coarse
Juice of 1 lemon, sieved
2 bay leaves
1 teaspoon salt
½ teaspoon white pepper

15

In a soup kettle, combine all the ingredients and simmer them, covered, for 30 minutes, or until the potato is very tender. Remove the bay leaves.

In the container of an electric blender, whirl the mixture, two cupfuls at a time, for 15 seconds, or until it is smooth. Transfer it to a large saucepan.

1 cup light cream, scalded

Add the cream and heat the soup, stirring, to blend the flavors.

Scallion Quiche

PREPARATION: 25 MINUTES

COOKING: 35 MINUTES IN A 400°/325° F. OVEN

The preparation time does not include readying the pastry.

One 9-inch pastry shell, page 237

Prepare the pastry.

3 tablespoons butter
2 large bunches scallions, trimmed and chopped, with as
**   much green as possible**

In a saucepan or skillet, heat the butter and in it cook the scallions, covered, for 5 minutes, or until they are wilted. Remove them from the heat and reserve them.

1 cup grated Gruyère cheese
1 cup grated Swiss cheese

In a mixing bowl, toss the cheeses together.

4 eggs	**½ teaspoon salt**
1½ cups light cream	**½ teaspoon white pepper**
Grating of nutmeg	

In a mixing bowl, beat the eggs lightly. Stir in the cream and seasonings.

At this point you may stop and continue later.

Prepared pastry shell
Reserved scallions

Over the bottom of the pastry shell, spread the scallions in an even layer. Over the scallions, sprinkle the cheese. Over the cheese, pour the custard. Bake the quiche at 400° for 15 minutes; reduce the heat to 325° and continue baking it for 20 minutes, or until the custard is set and the pastry is golden brown.

Carrots Glazed in Honey

DOUBLES / REFRIGERATES

PREPARATION: 20 MINUTES

3 tablespoons butter	Grating of nutmeg
6 large carrots, scraped and either cut into julienne strips or sliced thin	Salt Fresh-ground white pepper

In a skillet with a lid, heat the butter. Add the carrots and season them to taste. Over medium heat, stir the carrots to coat them well. Reduce the heat and cook, covered, stirring occasionally, for 10 minutes, or until the carrots are tender-crisp.

4 tablespoons honey

Into the carrots, stir the honey; cook, uncovered, stirring, until they are glazed. Transfer them, if desired, to an oven-proof serving dish.

At this point you may stop and continue later.

Fine-chopped parsley

Reheat the carrots, covered, in the oven. Garnish them with the chopped parsley.

Green Peas with Mint

DOUBLES

PREPARATION: 20 MINUTES

The preparation time does not include shelling the peas.

3 pounds fresh green peas or three 10-ounce packages frozen peas Soft sweet butter	Salt White pepper 3 or 4 fresh mint leaves, chopped fine

In boiling salted water, cook the peas, uncovered, for 12 minutes, or until they are just tender. Drain them, arrange them in a warm serving dish and add, to taste, butter, salt, pepper, and the mint.

Apricot Pudding

REFRIGERATES

PREPARATION: 45 MINUTES
CHILLING TIME: 6 HOURS

> 5 cups water
> 1 pound dried apricots
> 1 cup sugar
> Pinch of salt

In a saucepan, combine these four ingredients. Bring the liquid to the boil, reduce the heat, and simmer the apricots, covered, for 40 minutes, or until they are very soft.

   In the container of an electric blender, on medium speed, whirl the contents of the saucepan, 2 cups at a time, for 15 seconds, or until the purée is smooth. Transfer the purée to another saucepan.

> 1 tablespoon cornstarch, mixed with ¼ cup cold water
> Whipped cream or Custard Sauce, page 258 (optional)

To the purée, add the cornstarch. Over high heat, bring the pudding to the boil, stirring constantly; cook until it is thickened and smooth. Spoon it into a serving dish, allow it to cool, and chill it for at least 6 hours, or until it is set. If desired, serve it with whipped cream or custard sauce.

Fresh Pea Soup
Eggplant Rolls
Mixed Green Salad, page 245
Pears with Chocolate Sauce

FOR 4 PERSONS

Serve the soup hot or cold. The eggplant rolls, an import from Italy, may, if desired, be made with Mornay Sauce, page 256, in place of tomato sauce. Because the main dish is not heavy, you may wish to make the salad abundant. Pears with chocolate sauce, *poires Hélène* in their native France, provide an unusual and tasty dessert.

Fresh Pea Soup

DOUBLES / REFRIGERATES / FREEZES

PREPARATION: 45 MINUTES

    3 tablespoons butter
    1 cup shredded lettuce
    1 medium onion, peeled and chopped

In a large saucepan, heat the butter and in it cook the lettuce and onion, covered, until the onion is translucent.

    3 cups fresh young peas   4 or 5 fresh mint leaves, chopped
       (or 2 packages frozen   (or 1 teaspoon dried mint)
       peas)   1 teaspoon sugar
    3 cups water   Salt
    3 vegetable bouillon cubes Fresh-ground pepper

To the contents of the saucepan, add these seven ingredients. Cook, covered, for 25 minutes, or until the peas are very tender.

In the container of an electric blender, whirl the mixture on medium speed, 2 cups at a time, for 15 seconds, or until it is reduced to a smooth purée.

1 cup heavy cream, scalded

Add the scalded cream, stirring to blend the soup well. Adjust the seasoning if necessary.

Eggplant Rolls

DOUBLES

PREPARATION: 45 MINUTES
COOKING: 20 MINUTES IN A 350° F. OVEN

The preparation time does not include readying the tomato sauce.

Tomato Sauce, page 253

Prepare the sauce, and reserve.

Two 1-pound eggplants
Olive oil, into which 1 clove garlic has been pressed

Cut the eggplants lengthwise into ½-inch slices. Arrange them on a baking sheet, brush them with olive oil, and brown them under the broiler. Turn the slices, brush them with olive oil, and brown their reverse sides. Allow them to cool.

1½ cups ricotta cheese   **1 egg**
⅓ cup grated Parmesan cheese   **Salt**
1 clove garlic, pressed   **Fresh-ground pepper**
4 or 5 fresh basil leaves, chopped
**   (or ½ teaspoon dried oregano)**

In a mixing bowl, combine and blend the first five ingredients. Add salt and pepper to taste.

Spread the cheese mixture evenly over the eggplant slices. Starting at the narrow end, roll up each slice as you would a crêpe.

In a lightly oiled oven-proof serving dish, arrange the eggplant rolls in a single layer.

At this point you may stop and continue later.

Prepared tomato sauce

Over the rolls, pour the tomato sauce. Bake at 350° for 20 minutes, or until the sauce is bubbly.

Pears with Chocolate Sauce

DOUBLES / REFRIGERATES

PREPARATION: 20 MINUTES
COOKING: 1½ HOURS IN A 300° F. OVEN

    6 large firm pears, peeled

In a casserole, stand the pears.

    1 cup water
    ⅓ cup sugar
    Zest and sieved juice of 1 lemon
    Few grains of salt

In a saucepan, combine these five ingredients and bring them to the boil. Over the pears, pour the syrup; tuck the lemon zest among them. Bake the pears, covered at 300° for 1½ hours, or until they are tender. Baste them occasionally with the syrup and allow them to cool in it. Discard the lemon zest. Remove the pears to a serving dish, cover with plastic wrap and chill.

    While the pears are cooking, prepare the chocolate sauce.

    1½ cups milk
    2 ounces (2 squares) unsweetened chocolate

In the top of a double boiler over simmering water, combine the milk and chocolate; melt the chocolate.

    ½ cup sugar   1 teaspoon vanilla
    1 tablespoon flour   2 tablespoons butter (optional)
    Few grains of salt

In a small mixing bowl, sift together the sugar, flour, and salt. Stir the mixture into the chocolate milk and, over direct heat, cook the sauce,

stirring constantly until it is thickened and smooth. Stir in the vanilla
and butter, if desired.

The prepared sauce may be reheated in a double boiler to accompany
the chilled pears (I enjoy the contrasting temperatures), or it may be
served at room temperature.

Scallion Soup
Spinach-filled Crêpes
Carrots Glazed in Honey, page 17
Bean Sprout, Water Chestnut, and Onion Salad
Fresh Pineapple with Ginger

FOR 6 PERSONS

How tempting spinach can be, combined with healthful ricotta cheese
and elegantly presented encased in crêpes! A fine *pièce de résistance*
to follow the delicate soup. The carrots look well with the crêpes, while
the salad provides an unusual combination of tastes and textures. I
enjoy the tang the ginger gives pineapple; choose a very ripe one for
this dessert.

Scallion Soup

DOUBLES / REFRIGERATES / FREEZES

PREPARATION: 40 MINUTES

*If desired, the soup may be enriched by using half-and-half or light
cream in place of the milk. But for this particular menu, I feel a lighter
first course is preferable.*

3 bunches (about 2 dozen)   8 sprigs parsley
  scallions, trimmed and   2 bay leaves
  chopped with as much   3 cups water
  green as is firm   4 vegetable bouillon cubes
1 medium potato, peeled
  and chopped

In a large saucepan, combine the scallions, potato, parsley, and bay
leaves. Add the water and bouillon cubes. Bring the liquid to the boil,
reduce the heat, and simmer the vegetables, covered for 30 minutes, or
until the potato is very tender. Remove the bay leaves.

In the container of an electric blender, whirl the mixture on medium
speed, two cups at a time, for 15 seconds, or until it is reduced to a
smooth purée.

3 cups milk, scalded
Salt
Fresh-ground white pepper
Dill weed

To the scalded milk, add the purée, stirring to blend the soup. Adjust
the seasoning to taste. Garnish the soup with a sprinkling of dill weed.

Spinach-filled Crêpes

DOUBLES / REFRIGERATES

PREPARATION: 1½ HOURS
COOKING: 12 TO 15 MINUTES IN A 400° F. OVEN

Prepare 18 crêpes, page 239.

Prepare the filling:

Two 10-ounce packages fresh spinach, the woody stems removed, well rinsed, wilted (page 36), and chopped fine
(or two 10-ounce packages frozen chopped spinach,
fully thawed to room temperature)

In a colander or heavy sieve, press the chopped spinach as dry as
possible.

2 eggs   Salt
1¼ cups Ricotta cheese   Fresh-ground pepper
½ cup grated Parmesan cheese

In a mixing bowl, beat the eggs lightly. Add the Ricotta and Parmesan cheeses and blend the mixture well. Add salt and pepper to taste.

1 small onion, grated

To the egg mixture, add the spinach and onion. Blend the filling well. Spread a little of the filling on each of the prepared crêpes. Roll them and arrange them, smooth side up, in a lightly buttered oven-proof serving dish.

3 cups Mornay Sauce, page 256

Prepare the sauce and spoon it evenly over the crêpes.

At this point you may stop and continue later. (If you plan to continue later, cover the dish tightly with plastic wrap.)

Bake the crêpes, uncovered, at 400° for 12 minutes, or until the sauce is bubbly.

Bean Sprout, Water Chestnut, and Onion Salad

DOUBLES / REFRIGERATES

PREPARATION: 15 MINUTES
CHILLING TIME: 2 HOURS

Fresh bean sprouts are increasingly available and are superior to canned ones.

2 packages fresh bean sprouts   1 medium red onion, peeled
   or one 16-ounce can,   and sliced, the rings
   drained   separated
One 8-ounce can water chest-   Vinaigrette Sauce, page 254
   nuts, drained and sliced

In a salad bowl, combine the first three ingredients and dress them to taste with the vinaigrette dressing. Chill the salad for at least 2 hours.

Fresh Pineapple with Ginger

Prepare a fresh, ripe pineapple as directed on page 156. Toss it with 3 tablespoons preserved (candied) ginger, chopped fine, a light sprinkling of powdered ginger, and, if desired, ¼ cup of some aromatic liqueur, such as Italian Strega or Galliano. Cover the pineapple and allow it to macerate in the refrigerator for at least 3 hours.

Eggs in Tarragon Aspic
Cabbage with Cheese Sauce
Cornbread, page 236
Asparagus Salad
Fresh Pineapple with Ginger, page 25

FOR 6 PERSONS

Eggs in aspic! A glamorous make-ahead appetizer coupled, in this menu, with a seemingly homely cabbage; but here the cabbage is glamorized, too, and complemented by cornbread. I should be President of the National Asparagus Club—if such there were—so fond am I of this handsome vegetable; no way of serving it pleases me more than that suggested here.

Eggs in Tarragon Aspic

DOUBLES / REFRIGERATES

PREPARATION: 35 MINUTES
CHILLING TIME: 6 HOURS

Tarragon, one of my favorite herbs, grows in a big fat clump outside my kitchen door; guests find that they meet it often at my dining table.

Traditionally, eggs in aspic are made with a perfectly shaped poached egg resting in the gelatin; but even in Paris restaurants I have enjoyed them soft-boiled and peeled, imbedded in their quivering nest. Shelling a soft-boiled egg is tricky, but if you are successful you are assured an eye-appealing appetizer.

2 cups boiling water
1 envelope plus 1 teaspoon
   unflavored gelatin, softened in ¼ cup cold water
2 vegetable bouillon cubes

1 tablespoon fresh tarragon
   leaves, bruised (or 2 teaspoons dried tarragon)
¼ teaspoon salt

To the boiling water, add the remaining ingredients and stir the mixture until the gelatin and bouillon cubes are dissolved. Cover the liquid and allow the tarragon to infuse for 30 minutes.

6 small eggs, boiled for 4 to 5 minutes

Meanwhile, boil the eggs, immerse them in cold water, peel them carefully, and reserve.

2 tablespoons Madeira (or dry sherry)

Into the cooled gelatin, stir the Madeira or sherry.

12 leaves fresh tarragon (or 6 leaves parsley)

In 6 individual 4-ounce ramekins, arrange the tarragon leaves, crossed, or the parsley. Over the leaves, sieve about ¼ inch of gelatin. Chill the ramekins until the gelatin is nearly set.

Reserved eggs

In each ramekin, arrange an egg. Sieve the remaining gelatin equally into the six dishes. Chill them for at least 6 hours, or until the aspic is set. At the time of serving, unmold the ramekins with the leaves on top onto individual plates.

Cabbage with Cheese Sauce

DOUBLES / REFRIGERATES

PREPARATION: 25 MINUTES

COOKING: 10 MINUTES IN A 400° F. OVEN

1 large head cabbage, cut into six wedges

In boiling salted water to cover, cook the cabbage, covered, for 10 minutes, or until it is just tender. Drain and arrange it, with as much of the cut surface exposed as possible, in a lightly buttered oven-proof serving dish.

4 tablespoons butter	Grating of nutmeg
4 tablespoons flour	Fresh-ground pepper
2 cups milk	

In a saucepan, heat the butter and in it, over gentle heat, cook the flour for a few minutes. Gradually add the milk, stirring constantly until the mixture is thickened and smooth. Stir in the nutmeg, salt, and pepper.

1½ cups coarse-grated Cheddar cheese

Away from the heat, add the cheese, stirring until it is melted. Over the cabbage, pour the sauce.

At this point you may stop and continue later. (If you plan to continue later, cover the dish tightly with plastic wrap.)

Bake the cabbage at 400° for 10 minutes, or until the sauce is bubbly.

Asparagus Salad

DOUBLES / REFRIGERATES

Prepare and cook 24 to 30 stalks of asparagus as directed on page 52. Dress the asparagus with Vinaigrette Sauce, page 254, or Soy Dressing, page 257, and chill the salad for 2 hours before serving it.

Spinach Noodles with Mushroom Sauce
Green Salad, page 245, with Guacamole
Cold Lemon Soufflé

FOR 4 PERSONS

One of the most flavorful pasta dishes I know—and one of the most attractive to look at—is spinach macaroni (more often called green noodles) with mushroom sauce. Serve the guacamole on a bed of crisp greens; it makes a delicious salad. The soufflé, light and tangy, is a pleasant ending to the meal. You will notice that everything except boiling the pasta may be done in advance.

Spinach Noodles with Mushroom Sauce

DOUBLES / REFRIGERATES

PREPARATION: 35 MINUTES
COOKING: 8 MINUTES

> 3 tablespoons butter
> 4 medium onions, peeled and sliced

In a saucepan, heat the butter and in it, over gentle heat, cook the onions, covered, for 20 minutes, or until they are very tender.

> 4 tablespoons butter   Salt
> 2 pounds mushrooms, sliced   Fresh-ground pepper
> Grating of nutmeg

In a second saucepan, heat the butter and in it, over gentle heat, cook the mushrooms, covered, for 10 minutes, or until they are tender. Season them to taste.

1½ cups heavy cream
Cooked onion

In the container of an electric blender, combine the cream and the onion. On medium speed, whirl the mixture for 15 seconds, or until it is smooth.

To the mushrooms, add the onion mixture, stirring to blend the sauce well. Add more cream, if necessary, to give the sauce the desired consistency. Adjust the seasoning.

At this point you may stop and continue later.

1 pound spinach macaroni
("green noodles")

In a soup kettle, bring several quarts of salted water to the rolling boil. Add the noodles and boil it for 8 minutes, or until it is cooked *al dente* —tender but still with body. Drain it in a colander and rinse it with very hot water.

Grated Parmesan cheese
Fresh-ground black pepper

On warmed plates, arrange the noodles in equal servings. Over the noodles, ladle a generous serving of the mushroom sauce, which has been brought to room temperature over gentle heat. Offer the cheese and pepper mill separately.

Guacamole

DOUBLES / REFRIGERATES

PREPARATION: 20 MINUTES
CHILLING TIME: 2 HOURS

2 large ripe avocados, peeled, seeded, and chopped coarse
1 large onion, peeled, and chopped fine
1 medium ripe tomato, peeled, seeded, and chopped
Juice of 1 lime

In a mixing bowl, combine these four ingredients and, using a fork, mash and blend them (the guacamole should *not* be completely smooth).

Tabasco
Salt

Season the mixture with a drop or two of Tabasco and salt to taste. Chill the guacamole, covered, for at least 2 hours.

Cold Lemon Soufflé

DOUBLES / REFRIGERATES

PREPARATION: 30 MINUTES
CHILLING TIME: 6 HOURS

Wrap a 1½-quart soufflé dish with a 3-inch collar of foil, lightly oiled; or, if you prefer, use a 2-quart soufflé dish or other serving bowl, without the collar. Chill the utensil.

1¾ cups milk
4 egg yolks

In the top of a double boiler, over direct heat, bring the milk to the boil. In a mixing bowl large enough to hold the milk, lightly beat the egg yolks. Over the yolks, pour the boiling milk, beating the mixture constantly. Return it to the top of the double boiler, and place over simmering water.

½ cup sugar

Add the sugar. Stir the mixture until it coats the spoon. Remove from heat.

1 envelope unflavored gelatin
Grated rind of 2 large lemons
½ cup fresh lemon juice, sieved

Add the gelatin, stirring the custard until the gelatin is dissolved. Stir in the lemon rind and juice. Chill the mixture until it is thick.

1 cup heavy cream, whipped
4 egg whites, beaten until stiff but not dry

Transfer the lemon custard to a large, chilled mixing bowl. Into it fold

first the cream and then, the egg white. Spoon the soufflé into the
prepared dish and chill it for at least 6 hours, or until it is set.

Baked Mushroom Canapés
Corn Soufflé, All-Seasons
Green Peas à la Française
Mixed Salad, page 247
Assorted Cheese and Fresh Fruit, page 248

FOR 4 PERSONS

You probably will not have corn from your garden at this time of year;
if you do, use the Corn Soufflé recipe on page 104. But you may well
have early fresh peas; in this case, treat them lovingly, cooking them in
the classic French way in order to reserve their sweetness. Put quite a
lot of watercress in the salad. And then a ripe Brie with fresh fruit of
your choice.

Baked Mushroom Canapés

DOUBLES / REFRIGERATES PRIOR TO BAKING

PREPARATION: 30 MINUTES
COOKING: 15 MINUTES IN A 350° F. OVEN

24 medium, well formed mushrooms	Sour cream
	Salt
1 small onion, peeled and chopped fine	Fresh-ground pepper

Remove the stems of the mushrooms, trim the bottom ends, and
chop the stems fine. In a mixing bowl, combine the chopped stems

and onion and add just enough sour cream to bind the mixture. Season to taste with salt and pepper.

Melted butter (or Vinaigrette Sauce, page 254)

In the melted butter, dip the mushroom caps one at a time until each is coated (the amount of butter required will depend upon the size of the mushrooms).

Paprika

Fill the caps with the mushroom stem mixture. Garnish each with a sprinkling of paprika.

6 pieces buttered toast, the crusts removed

On each piece of the toast, arrange 4 of the mushroom caps, smooth side down.

At this point you may stop and continue later. (Also at this point the mushrooms may be refrigerated.)

On an oven-proof serving dish, arrange the toast squares and bake the mushrooms at 350° for 15 minutes, or until they are tender.

Corn Soufflé, All-Seasons

PREPARATION: 15 MINUTES
COOKING: 30 MINUTES IN A 350° F. OVEN

All ingredients for the soufflé, and its dish, may be readied in advance.

4 tablespoons butter
4 tablespoons flour

In a saucepan, heat the butter and in it, over gentle heat, cook the flour, stirring, for a few minutes.

½ cup milk
One 17-ounce can creamed-style corn
Grating of nutmeg
Salt

Gradually add the milk and then the corn, stirring until the mixture is thickened and smooth. Add nutmeg and salt, to taste.

At this point you may stop and continue later.

4 egg yolks

Off heat, beat in the egg yolks.

4 egg whites, beaten until stiff but not dry

Into corn mixture, fold the egg white. Spoon the batter into a lightly buttered 2-quart soufflé dish. Bake the soufflé at 350° for 30 minutes, or until it is well puffed and golden.

Green Peas à la Française

PREPARATION: 25 MINUTES
COOKING: 1 HOUR IN A 350° F. OVEN

Bake the peas in the lower part of the oven, starting them 30 minutes before the soufflé.

1 head Boston lettuce, rinsed, some excess water removed, and shredded	2 scallions, trimmed and chopped fine with some of the firm green part
2 pounds green peas, shelled and rinsed under cold water (or two 10-ounce packages frozen peas)	Butter Salt Fresh-ground white pepper

In an oven-proof serving dish, arrange one half the lettuce in an even layer. Over the lettuce, arrange the peas in an even layer; over the peas, sprinkle the scallions. Dot with butter and season with salt and pepper to taste. Arrange a layer of the remaining lettuce over all. Cover the dish tightly.

At this point you may stop and continue later.

Bake at 350° for 1 hour. You will find that the lettuce has virtually disappeared into a sort of sauce and that the peas are plump and tender.

Asparagus Parmesan
Baked Potatoes with Aioli Sauce
Wilted Spinach
Bananas Flambés

FOR 6 PERSONS

The asparagus, more than an appetizer, is a full course in itself. I have always felt that a potato well baked is a dish fit for both kings and gods; I think you will enjoy the novelty of serving it with *aioli* sauce. Offer the spinach as a cooked salad. The bananas, flaming and flavorful, are particularly dramatic, especially if prepared in a chafing dish at table.

Asparagus Parmesan

DOUBLES

PREPARATION: 12 MINUTES
COOKING: 20 MINUTES IN A 350° F. OVEN

> **36 stalks fat asparagus**
> **Salt**
> **Pepper**
> **Grated Parmesan cheese**

Cut the asparagus just to fit a large flat oven-proof serving dish. With a vegetable peeler, lightly peel the heavy stalk to within 3 or 4 inches of the tip. Rinse the stalks in cold water and arrange them in the dish, gently shaking off only excess water. Sprinkle with a little salt and pepper and then, more generously, with the cheese, to taste. Cover the dish tightly with aluminum foil.

At this point you may stop and continue later. (If you are going to wait several hours before cooking the asparagus, refrigerate it.)

6 lemon wedges

Bake the asparagus at 350° for 20 minutes, or until it is tender-crisp. Serve it with the lemon wedges.

Baked Potatoes with Aioli Sauce

DOUBLES

PREPARATION: 5 MINUTES
COOKING: 1¼ HOURS IN A 350° F. OVEN

The preparation time does not include preparing the Aioli Sauce, page 251 (about 10 minutes).

Do not wrap the potatoes in foil; under these circumstances, they are steamed, not baked, and both taste and consistency are changed. For the calorie-conscious, rubbing the potatoes with butter may be omitted; and sour cream with coarsely chopped garlic cloves, to taste, whirled in the container of an electric blender is less rich than *aioli*. Of course, traditional butter, crisp bacon bits, and chopped chives also provide a tasty garnish.

6 large Idaho potatoes, scrubbed and dried with absorbent paper
Soft butter

With the tines of a fork, puncture the potatoes in several places to allow steam to escape. With a little butter, rub each potato to cover it smoothly (this will render the skin crisp, the best part of a baked potato). Arrange the potatoes on a baking sheet.

At this point you may stop and continue later.

Bake the potatoes at 350° for 1¼ hours, or until they are fork-tender. (If you are not serving the asparagus, or if you have two ovens, the potatoes may be baked at 400° for 1 hour or at 450° for 40 minutes.)

Aioli Sauce, page 251

Serve the sauce separately, at room temperature, and pass salt and a well-operating pepper mill.

Wilted Spinach

DOUBLES / REFRIGERATES

PREPARATION: 15 MINUTES

Three 10-ounce packages fresh spinach, the woody stems removed, washed in cold water

In a large soup kettle, bring to the boil several quarts of slightly salted water. Into it, plunge the spinach, allowing the vegetable to wilt for only 20 seconds. Drain it at once.

Oil-and-Lemon Dressing, page 256

In a large bowl, arrange the spinach, and, with two forks, gently toss it with the dressing, using your desired amount; the salad should not be oily. Chill the spinach until you are nearly ready to serve it; its flavor is improved when it is cool but not taken directly from the refrigerator.

Bananas Flambés

PREPARATION: 10 MINUTES
COOKING: 6 MINUTES

2 tablespoons butter	Juice of 1 lemon
½ cup brown sugar	½ teaspoon cinnamon
½ cup orange juice	1 teaspoon vanilla

In a skillet or, if desired, in a chafing dish, combine these ingredients and bring them to the boil. Reduce the heat.

6 large firm ripe bananas, peeled, halved both length- and crosswise, and "painted" with lemon juice (this will prevent their darkening before being cooked)

In the simmering poaching syrup, cook the bananas, a few at a time, if necessary, for 1 minute on each side, or until they are slightly soft. Remove them to a warm flame-proof serving dish.

½ cup orange-flavored liqueur

Over high heat, reduce the syrup slightly; pour it over the bananas. In the skillet, warm the liqueur, ignite it, and pour it over the bananas. When the flame dies, serve four banana pieces to each person.

Baked Mushroom Canapés, page 31
Asparagus Soufflé
Spinach with Croutons
Lemon Meringue Pie

FOR 4 PERSONS

A menu for early spring, when we all think about asparagus, but when it is costly to indulge our yearning. This unusual soufflé is an economical way to satisfy that emotional void and, happily, the appetite as well. Lemon meringue, recalling memories of childhood and happy family dinners, is *perhaps* my favorite pie.

_____

Asparagus Soufflé

PREPARATION: 25 MINUTES
COOKING: 30 MINUTES IN A 350° F. OVEN

All ingredients for the soufflé, and its dish, may be readied in advance.

Two 10-ounce packages frozen cut asparagus, fully thawed to
　　　room temperature
¼ cup milk

In the container of an electric blender, combine the asparagus and milk and, on medium speed, whirl them for 15 seconds, or until the mixture is smooth. Reserve it.

4 tablespoons butter
4 tablespoons flour
1 vegetable bouillon cube, powdered

In a large saucepan, heat the butter and in it, over gentle heat, cook the flour for a few minutes. Stir in the bouillon powder.

At this point you may stop and continue later.

Reserved asparagus mixture   4 egg yolks
¼ cup grated Parmesan   Salt
  cheese   Fresh-ground white pepper

To the hot *roux*, gradually add the asparagus mixture, stirring constantly until thickened and smooth. Away from the heat, stir in the cheese and beat in the egg yolks. Adjust the seasoning to taste.

4 egg whites, beaten until stiff but not dry

Into the asparagus mixture, fold the egg whites. Spoon into a lightly buttered 2-quart soufflé dish and bake at 350° for 30 minutes, or until the soufflé is well puffed and golden.

Spinach with Croutons

Follow the directions for Wilted Spinach, page 36, and add to the prepared vegetable ½ to ¾ cup croutons, toasted in olive oil in which a garlic clove, peeled and sliced, has been sautéed.

Lemon Meringue Pie

REFRIGERATES

PREPARATION: 30 MINUTES
COOKING: 5 MINUTES IN A 425° F. OVEN

If desired, you may make individual lemon tarts by lining muffin cups with the pastry.

The preparation time does not include readying the pastry.

One 9-inch pastry shell (or 6 tart shells), fully baked, page 237

Prepare the pastry.

4 tablespoons flour
4 tablespoons cornstarch
1½ cups sugar
½ teaspoon salt

In the top of a double boiler, combine and blend these four ingredients.

1½ cups water

To the contents of the double boiler, add the water and, over medium heat, cook the mixture, stirring constantly, until it boils. Over boiling water, cook it, covered, for 20 minutes.

1 tablespoon butter
Grated rind of 1 lemon
⅓ cup fresh lemon juice, sieved
4 egg yolks

Add these four ingredients, beating vigorously to blend the mixture well. Over boiling water, cook it, stirring, until thick. Allow it to cool. Spoon the cooked lemon custard into the prepared pastry shell.

4 egg whites
4 tablespoons sugar
1 teaspoon lemon juice

In a mixing bowl, beat the egg whites until they stand in soft peaks. Gradually add the sugar and then the lemon juice, beating constantly, until the meringue is very stiff.

Spoon the meringue over the lemon custard. Bake the pie at 425° for 5 minutes, or until the meringue is lightly browned.

Vegetable Chow Mein
Rice, page 239
Asparagus Salad, page 27
Exotic Fruits in Gelatin
Oatmeal Cookies, page 250

FOR 6 PERSONS

The menu is pseudo-Chinese, save for the cookies—which emphatically are not!

Vegetable Chow Mein

DOUBLES

PREPARATION: 20 MINUTES
COOKING: 15 MINUTES

This dish refrigerates only for use as leftovers; the textures tend to be lost with reheating.

4 tablespoons oil	3 medium carrots, scraped and
6 scallions trimmed and	sliced thin
chopped on the bias	1 green or sweet red pepper,
½ medium head cabbage,	seeded and cut in julienne
shredded fine (about	strips
3 cups	1 tablespoon pale dry sherry
3 stalks celery, cut in	2 tablespoons soy sauce
½-inch pieces on the	1 teaspoon sugar
bias (about 1 cup)	¼ teaspoon pepper

In a large skillet or wok, heat the oil. To it, add the vegetables and seasonings. Over high heat, stir-fry the vegetables for 5 minutes.

1 cup hot water, in which 3 vegetable bouillon cubes are
   dissolved
Soy sauce

Season the bouillon with soy sauce, to taste. Add the liquid to the
vegetables and continue to cook them, covered, for 5 minutes, or until
they are barely tender-crisp.

At this point you may stop and continue later.

2 tablespoons cornstarch
1 cup cold water
Soy sauce

Stir the cornstarch into the cold water. Add the mixture to the vegetables and, over high heat, stir the chow mein for 3 minutes, or until
the sauce is thickened and smooth. Adjust the seasoning with soy sauce
to taste.

Exotic Fruits in Gelatin

DOUBLES / REFRIGERATES

PREPARATION: 20 MINUTES
CHILLING TIME: 6 HOURS

2 tablespoons preserved ginger, chopped fine
One 1-pound can lichee nuts
One 1-pound can sliced mango

In a 1½-quart ring mold, arrange the ginger. Drain the nuts, reserving
the liquid, and arrange them in the mold. Drain the mango, reserving
the liquid, and arrange it over the lichees.

Reserved liquid from fruits
Lemon juice, sieved to taste

Sieve and combine the liquids in a saucepan. Add lemon juice to taste
until the liquid has a slight piquancy.

1½ envelopes unflavored gelatin

Over the liquid, sprinkle the gelatin and allow it to soften. Over
medium heat, stir the liquid until the gelatin is dissolved. Pour the

liquid into the ring mold. Refrigerate the dessert for at least 6 hours, or until it is set.

Custard Sauce, page 258

Unmold the dessert and serve it with the sauce.

Potato Soup
Eggs Baked in Sweet Peppers
Braised Endive
Muffins, page 235
Strawberry Tart

FOR 6 PERSONS

If you wish, make the soup of new potatoes; depending upon their size, equate 3 new potatoes with 1 medium potato as called for in the recipe. Wash the new potatoes well but do not remove their skins. Garnish the soup with fine-chopped scallions. If desired, the tart may be made with graham-cracker crumb crust, a pleasant change from short pastry.

Potato Soup

DOUBLES / REFRIGERATES / FREEZES

PREPARATION: 30 MINUTES
COOKING: 1 HOUR

Potage Parmentier is named for the gentleman who, in the eighteenth century, popularized in France the theretofore unpopular potato; he even prevailed upon King Louis XVI to eat them. Since then, the French have thrived on potatoes cooked in countless delicious ways of their culinary invention.

1 pound potatoes, peeled
  and chopped
2 large onions, peeled and
  chopped
2 leeks, well rinsed and
  chopped (if leeks are unavailable, use 6 scallions)

1 large carrot, scraped
  and chopped
8 cups water
4 vegetable bouillon
  cubes
½ teaspoon pepper

In a soup kettle, combine these ingredients. Bring the liquid to the boil, reduce the heat, and simmer the vegetables, covered, for 1 hour, or until they are very tender.

In the container of an electric blender, whirl the potato mixture, 2 cups at a time, until it is smooth. Transfer it to a large saucepan.

4 tablespoons soft butter
½ cup heavy cream, scalded
Salt
1 cup fine-chopped parsley

To the soup, add the butter, stirring to melt it. Stir in the cream and season with salt to taste. Add the parsley, reserving only enough to garnish the soup at the time of serving it. Reheat the soup over gentle heat, stirring it often.

If the soup is thicker than you wish, thin it to the desired consistency with milk.

Eggs Baked in Sweet Peppers

PREPARATION: 20 MINUTES
COOKING: 20 MINUTES IN A 350° F. OVEN

3 firm, well-shaped sweet green peppers

Remove the stems and then cut the peppers in half lengthwise. Blanch them for 5 minutes in boiling salted water. Refresh them in cold water and drain them well.

3 tablespoons butter
1 medium onion, peeled and
    grated
2 cups poultry stuffing
1 cup Tomato Sauce, page
    253, or 1 8-ounce can
    tomato sauce

Pinch of thyme
Salt
Fresh-ground pepper

In a skillet, heat the butter and in it cook the onion until translucent. To the onion, add the stuffing, stirring to blend the mixture well. Stir in the tomato sauce and season the mixture to taste.

6 small eggs
Paprika

Spoon the stuffing mixture equally into the pepper shells. Arrange them in an oven-proof baking dish. Into each, break an egg. Sprinkle each with paprika.

At this point you may stop and continue later.

Bake the peppers, covered, at 350° for 20 minutes, or until the eggs are just set.

Braised Endive

PREPARATION: 10 MINUTES
COOKING: 20 MINUTES

6 large Belgian endive, trimmed and split lengthwise
1 cup dry white wine (or water)
1 vegetable bouillon cube, powdered

In a skillet with a lid, arrange the endive, split side up. Over them, pour the wine and sprinkle the bouillon powder.

At this point you may stop and continue later.

Bring the liquid rapidly to the boil, reduce the heat, and simmer the endive, covered, for 15 minutes. Increase the heat to medium-high, turn the endive, and cook them, uncovered, for 5 minutes longer, or until they are tender and the liquid is reduced and slightly thickened.

Strawberry Tart

REFRIGERATES

PREPARATION: 30 MINUTES
CHILLING TIME: 4 HOURS

The preparation time does not include readying the pastry.

One fully baked 8-inch pastry shell, page 237

Prepare the pastry.

| One 9-ounce package frozen strawberries, fully thawed to room temperature | 2 tablespoons cornstarch ½ cup sugar Few grains salt |

In the container of an electric blender, combine these four ingredients and, on medium speed, whirl them for 15 seconds, or until they are reduced to a smooth purée. In a saucepan, over medium heat, cook the purée, stirring constantly, until it is thickened and smooth. Allow the mixture to cool.

1 quart strawberries, hulled, rinsed in cold water, and drained on absorbent paper

Prepare the strawberries and reserve them.

| One 8-ounce package cream cheese, at room temperature ¾ cup heavy cream | ¼ cup orange-flavored liqueur 3 tablespoons sugar Few grains of salt |

In a mixing bowl, combine these five ingredients and, using a rotary beater, blend them well.

In the prepared pastry shell, arrange the cream cheese mixture in an even layer. Stud the entire surface with the reserved strawberries, pushing their stem ends slightly into the cheese mixture. Over the strawberries, spoon evenly the cooled cornstarch mixture. Chill the tart for at least 4 hours.

Asparagus, page 34
Mushrooms Chantilly
Carrots Vichy
Green Bean Salad
Gold Plum Soufflé

FOR 4 PERSONS

Serve the asparagus hot or cold with Vinaigrette Sauce, page 254. The mushrooms, a particularly tasty dish, look well in patty shells but are no less appetizing served on buttered toast (made of *very* good bread, the crusts removed). The soufflé recipe may be adapted to other canned fruits of your choice: prunes, peaches, apricots.

Mushrooms Chantilly

DOUBLES / REFRIGERATES

PREPARATION: 15 MINUTES
COOKING: 10 MINUTES

> 4 tablespoons butter
> 1 pound mushrooms, sliced

In a skillet with a lid, heat the butter and to it add the mushrooms, stirring to coat them well (more butter may be added, if necessary). Over medium heat, cook them, covered, for 2 minutes.

> ⅓ cup fine-chopped parsley
> Salt
> Fresh-ground pepper

Add the parsley and salt and pepper to taste. Over gentle heat, continue to cook the mushrooms, covered, for 5 minutes.

At this point you may stop and continue later.

1 cup heavy cream

Add the cream and, over medium heat, simmer the mushrooms, uncovered, for 10 minutes, or until the cream is somewhat thickened.

Carrots Vichy

DOUBLES / REFRIGERATES

PREPARATION: 25 MINUTES
COOKING: 10 MINUTES

Allow one very large or two small carrots per serving. They should be cut into medium julienne strips, not like match sticks (if cut too thin, they disintegrate when cooked).

Carrots
Boiling salted water

With a vegetable peeler, lightly peel the carrots. Using a very sharp and heavy knife (doing so reduces your work), cut the carrots as suggested above. In the boiling water, blanch them for 3 minutes. Refresh them in cold water. Drain them thoroughly.

6 tablespoons butter	½ teaspoon salt
½ cup dry vermouth	¼ teaspoon white pepper
2 teaspoons sugar	

In a large skillet, melt the butter and in it, toss the carrots, coating them well. Over them, sprinkle the vermouth and seasonings.

At this point you may stop and continue later.

¼ cup fine-chopped parsley

Over high heat, cook the carrots, shaking them often, for 10 minutes, or until the liquid evaporates. (If desired, the carrots may be cooked ahead and reheated at the time of serving.) Adjust the seasoning to taste. Serve the carrots sprinkled with the parsley.

Green Bean Salad

DOUBLES / REFRIGERATES

PREPARATION: 30 MINUTES
CHILLING TIME: 3 HOURS

*Beans fresh from either garden or supermarket have more taste, I feel,
if lightly cooked and served slightly chilled; their texture, too, is more
interesting when they are prepared this way.*

> 1½ pounds fresh green beans, the stems removed, halved,
> and rinsed in cold water

In a soup kettle, bring to a rolling boil several quarts of salted water.
Into it, plunge the beans; leave them uncovered. After the water has
returned to the boil, cook the beans for 12 minutes, or until they are
tender-crisp. (The age of the beans will determine their cooking time.)
Refresh them in cold water; drain and dry them on absorbent paper.

> Salad Dressing of your choice, pages 256–257
> ⅓ cup fine-chopped parsley or sprinkling of dill weed

In a large shallow bowl or deep platter, arrange the beans all pointing
the same way. Over them pour the dressing of your choice and sprinkle
them with one of the herbs. Cover the salad and refrigerate it for at
least 3 hours.

Gold Plum Soufflé

REFRIGERATES

PREPARATION: 30 MINUTES
CHILLING TIME: 6 HOURS

> One 16-ounce can purple plums

Drain the plums and reserve the liquid. Remove the pits and measure
1 cup, packed, of the plums. Reserve them.

> ½ cup plum liquid
> 1 envelope unflavored gelatin

In the plum liquid, soften the gelatin. Over hot water, dissolve it.

Sieved juice of ½ medium lemon
½ teaspoon vanilla
Few grains of salt

In the container of an electric blender, combine the dissolved gelatin, the reserved plums, and the seasonings. On medium speed, whirl the ingredients for 15 seconds, or until they are reduced to a smooth purée. Chill the mixture until it is the consistency of egg white.

4 egg whites
⅓ cup sugar

In a mixing bowl, beat the egg whites until they stand in soft peaks. Gradually add the sugar, beating constantly, until the egg whites are stiff.

Custard Sauce, page 258

Into the plum purée, fold the egg whites. Spoon the mixture into a 2-quart soufflé dish and chill it for at least 6 hours, or until it is set. Serve the soufflé with custard sauce.

Leeks in Piquant Sauce
Asparagus with Egg and Browned Butter
Muffins, page 235
Mixed Salad, page 247
Exotic Fruits in Gelatin, page 41

FOR 6 PERSONS

Serve the leeks hot or cold. The asparagus may be offered on toast (make the toast with very good bread!); in this case, you may want to omit the muffins. The salad should be a fairly substantial one, but the dressing should be plain, to contrast with the leeks. The dessert is something of a conversation piece, pretty to look at and unusual to taste.

Leeks in Piquant Sauce

DOUBLES / REFRIGERATES

PREPARATION: 20 MINUTES

>   12 leeks, trimmed and thoroughly rinsed under cold running
>   water
>   3 cups water in which 3 vegetable bouillon cubes are dis-
>   solved

In a large skillet with a lid, arrange the leeks; over them pour the bouillon. Bring the liquid rapidly to the boil, reduce the heat, and simmer the leeks, covered, for 15 minutes, or until they are tender.

Drain the leeks thoroughly. Allow them to cool and then refrigerate them, if desired; or arrange them in an oven-proof serving dish in order to reheat them at the time of serving.

>   Piquant Sauce, page 253

Over the leeks, pour the sauce. Serve the leeks cold or heat them at 400° for 10 minutes, or until the sauce is bubbly.

Asparagus with Egg and Browned Butter

DOUBLES

PREPARATION: 20 MINUTES
COOKING: 30 MINUTES IN A 350° F. OVEN

>   3 hard-boiled eggs

While the eggs are cooking, prepare the asparagus.

>   36 heavy spears fresh asparagus
>   Generous grating of nutmeg
>   Salt

Cut the asparagus to fit crosswise in an oven-proof serving dish. Using a vegetable peeler, peel the asparagus up to four inches from their base. Arrange them in the dish. Add a sprinkling of water and of nutmeg and salt. Cover the dish closely with foil.

8 tablespoons butter

In a small saucepan, melt the butter and, over gentle heat, stirring constantly, allow it to brown slightly. Reserve it.

1 bunch watercress, the woody stems removed, rinsed under cold water, drained and chopped

Prepare the watercress. Peel and chop the hard-boiled eggs. Cover the watercress and chill it.

At this point you may stop and continue later.

Bake the asparagus, covered, at 350° for 30 minutes. Reheat the browned butter and pour it into a heated pitcher.

Serve the asparagus on warmed plates and pass the butter, watercress, and eggs separately.

Baked Asparagus
Jerusalem Artichoke Pie
or
Mushrooms in Orange Sauce with Rice
Glazed Pearl Onions
Spinach Salad
Pears with Roquefort Cheese

FOR 4 PERSONS

Jerusalem artichokes are not readily found, hence an alternative *pièce de resistance* is offered. As a matter of fact, they are not artichokes at all, but the edible root of a species of sunflower called in Italy *girasole*; "Jerusalem artichoke" is a phonetic transliteration which has slipped into general usage. Like Jerusalem Artichoke Pie, Mushrooms in Orange Sauce are delicately flavored. The dessert, unusual and surprising, is light and may be made with any blue-veined cheese.

_____

Baked Asparagus

DOUBLES

PREPARATION: 10 MINUTES
COOKING: 20 MINUTES IN A 350° F. OVEN

This way of cooking asparagus is my own. I like it because it is easy and assures the preservation of both nutriments and flavor. For the purposes of this menu, bake the asparagus with the pie for the final 20 minutes of its cooking (see recipe for Jerusalem Artichoke Pie, below).

> 16 stalks *fat* asparagus
> Salt
> Fresh-ground pepper
> Sweet butter

Cut the asparagus just to fit a large flat oven-proof serving dish. With a vegetable peeler, lightly peel the heavy stalk to within 3 or 4 inches of the tip. Rinse the vegetable in cold water and arrange it in the dish, gently shaking off only the excess water. Sprinkle with salt and pepper and dot generously with butter. Cover the dish tightly with foil.

At this point you may stop and continue later. (If you are going to wait several hours before cooking the asparagus, refrigerate it.)

> 1 lemon, cut into lengthwise wedges

Bake the asparagus at 350° for 20 minutes, or until it is tender-crisp. Serve it with the lemon wedges.

Jerusalem Artichoke Pie

PREPARATION: 30 MINUTES
COOKING: 40 MINUTES IN A 350° F. OVEN

The preparation time does not include readying the pastry top crust.

Top crust of your choice (or use short pastry recipe, page 237)

Prepare the top crust.

1 pound Jerusalem artichokes, scrubbed and the knobs removed (peel them only if the skins seem tough)

In boiling salted water to cover, cook the Jerusalem artichokes for 8 minutes, or until they are just tender. Drain and slice them.

1 tablespoon butter	**Salt**
1 tablespoon flour	**Pepper**
1 cup milk	

In a saucepan, heat the butter and in it, over gentle heat, cook the flour, stirring, for a few minutes. Add the milk and cook the mixture, stirring constantly, until it is thickened and smooth. Season the sauce with salt and pepper to taste.

Reserved Jerusalem artichokes	**15 pitted dates, chopped coarse**
1 cup seedless grapes, stemmed, rinsed, and drained on absorbent paper	**¼ teaspoon mace**

Into the Béchamel stir these four ingredients. Transfer the mixture to a deep pie or soufflé dish.

Top crust of your choice

Arrange the top crust over the filling and bake the pie at 350° for 40 minutes, or until the crust is golden.

Mushrooms in Orange Sauce with Rice

DOUBLES / REFRIGERATES

PREPARATION: 30 MINUTES

> 6 tablespoons butter
> 1½ pounds mushrooms, quartered
> 1 teaspoon paprika

In a skillet or saucepan, heat the butter. Add the mushrooms and paprika; cook the mushrooms, covered, stirring them often, until they are nearly tender.

> 2½ tablespoons flour
> 1 medium onion, peeled and grated
> 1½ cups light cream (you may use milk, if desired)
> Grated rind and juice of 1 large orange
>
> ¼ cup fine-chopped parsley
> Grating of nutmeg
> Salt
> Fresh-ground pepper

Over the vegetables, sprinkle the flour. Add the onion and cream or milk and cook the mixture until the sauce is thickened and smooth. Stir in the orange rind, juice, parsley, and seasonings to taste. Serve the mushrooms with Rice, page 239.

Glazed Pearl Onions

DOUBLES / REFRIGERATES

PREPARATION: 15 MINUTES
COOKING: 15 MINUTES

If desired, the onions may be fully cooked and reheated at the time of serving.

> 3 tablespoons butter (or vegetable oil)
> 20 to 24 pearl (small white) onions, peeled

In a saucepan, heat the butter or oil and in it brown the onions, shaking the pan to coat them well.

¼ cup dry vermouth   Fresh-ground pepper
2 tablespoons vinegar   Salt
3 tablespoons brown sugar

Add the vermouth, vinegar, brown sugar, and seasonings. Simmer the onions, shaking the pan frequently, until the liquid is almost evaporated. (Prepared this way, the onions will be firm. For more tender onions, simmer them for 5 minutes, covered; remove the cover and proceed as directed.)

Spinach Salad

DOUBLES

PREPARATION: 15 MINUTES

A *pleasant addition: unflavored croutons (about 1 cup), sautéed in garlic-flavored olive oil.*

Two 10-ounce packages fresh spinach, the woody stems removed, washed in cold water

Dry the spinach in a salad drier or with absorbent paper. Cut or tear the leaves into manageable size. Refrigerate them until ready for use.

Vinaigrette Sauce, page 254

Toss the spinach with the sauce. (I feel that salad dressings should be at room temperature when added to chilled greens.)

Pears with Roquefort Cheese

DOUBLES / REFRIGERATES

PREPARATION: 25 MINUTES
COOKING: 5 MINUTES IN A 400° F. OVEN

If desired, you may use canned pear halves (one 29-ounce can); allow 2 halves per serving and reserve 1 cup of the syrup. In this case, eliminate step one.

4 firm pears, peeled, halved lengthwise, and cored

Using a simple syrup of 1 cup water and ⅓ cup sugar, poach the pear halves for 15 minutes; or until they are just tender.

½ cup (one 3-ounce package) Roquefort cheese, rolled into
    8 balls (any blue-veined cheese will do well)
3 tablespoons cognac
Grated rind and juice of ½ lemon

Arrange the pears, cavity side up, in a baking dish. In each cavity place a cheese ball. To either the simple syrup or canned pear liquid, add the cognac and lemon rind and juice. Pour the syrup over the pears.

At this point you may stop and continue later.

Bake the pears at 400° for 5 minutes, or until they are thoroughly heated.

Fresh Vegetable Soup
Corn Quiche
Dandelion Greens
             or
Fresh Spinach
Strawberries in Orange-Flavored Liqueur
Oatmeal Cookies, page 250

FOR 6 PERSONS

Spring cannot be allowed to pass without sampling the delicate flavor of vegetable soup made, perhaps, from the first yield of your garden.

The quiche is really a promise of things to come; for most of us, fresh corn is a late summer's harvest, but it is available earlier at the market, and frozen corn substitutes well. Early dandelion greens, if you can collect or buy them, are a short-lived seasonal treat, well worth the effort or search. And what could be more elegant than early strawberries in orange-flavored liqueur?

Fresh Vegetable Soup

DOUBLES / REFRIGERATES

PREPARATION: 45 MINUTES

½ cup olive oil
3 medium onions, peeled and sliced thin
1 clove garlic, chopped fine
3 large carrots, scraped and sliced thin
1 small cauliflower, cut into flowerets

6 scallions, chopped, with as much green as possible
3 ribs celery, chopped fine, with their leaves
1 small head Boston lettuce, chopped fine

In a soup kettle, heat the oil and in it cook the vegetables, stirring them often, until they are wilted.

4 cups water
2 cups dry white wine
4 vegetable bouillon cubes

1½ cups fresh peas or one 10-ounce package frozen peas
1 teaspoon salt
Fresh-ground pepper

To the vegetables, add the water, wine, and bouillon cubes; simmer the vegetables, covered, for 20 minutes. Add the peas and seasonings and continue to simmer the soup, covered, for 15 minutes, or until the peas are tender.

Fresh-grated Parmesan cheese

When serving the soup, offer the cheese separately.

Corn Quiche

PREPARATION: 15 MINUTES
COOKING: 45 MINUTES IN A 400°/350° F. OVEN

The preparation time does not include readying the pastry.

One 9-inch pastry shell, page 237

Prepare the pastry.

5 eggs
1½ cups light cream

In a mixing bowl, beat together the eggs and cream.

1½ cups uncooked fresh corn cut from the ear (or one 10-ounce package frozen corn kernels, fully thawed to room temperature)	1 medium onion, peeled and chopped fine ¼ cup grated Parmesan cheese ¾ teaspoon salt ¼ teaspoon white pepper

To the egg mixture, add these five ingredients, stirring to blend them well.

At this point you may stop and continue later.

Pour the filling into the prepared pastry shell. Bake the quiche at 400° for 25 minutes; reduce the heat to 350° and continue to bake it for 20 minutes, or until the pastry is golden and the custard is set. Allow the quiche to stand for 5 minutes before cutting it.

Dandelion Greens or Fresh Spinach

Gather 1¼ to 1½ pounds young dandelion greens; remove any woody stems, rinse them thoroughly in cold water, and cook them according to the directions for Spinach, page 36. If you buy dandelion greens, three bunches will suffice—or two 10-ounce bags of fresh spinach.

Strawberries in Orange-Flavored Liqueur

PREPARATION: 15 MINUTES
CHILLING TIME: 3 HOURS

1 quart strawberries

Hull, rinse, and drain the strawberries. If desired, halve them; I always do so with large berries.

Orange-flavored liqueur

Add, to taste, as much liqueur as you wish; I use about ⅓ to ½ cup. Gently toss the berries with the liqueur and refrigerate them for at least 3 hours.

Gazpacho
Avocado Mousse with Mixed Vegetable Salad
Orange and Whole Wheat Muffins, page 236
Pineapple Flambé
Oatmeal Cookies (optional), page 250

FOR 6 PERSONS

Because everything may be prepared or readied in advance, this menu appeals to me when expecting—at an unknown hour—weekend guests or when planning to work a long day in my spring garden. Because it is a cold meal, it serves equally well for summer fare.

Gazpacho

DOUBLES / REFRIGERATES

PREPARATION: 30 MINUTES

CHILLING TIME: 3 HOURS

Mexican? Portuguese? Gazpacho, actually of Spanish origin, is so inter-nationally known that most directions for making it are composites of several recipes. The following is my synthesis.

2 medium cucumbers,
  peeled, if desired,
  seeded, and diced
1 large red onion, peeled
  and chopped fine
1 green pepper, seeded and
  chopped fine
1 sweet red pepper, seeded
  and chopped fine
  (optional)

6 ripe tomatoes, peeled,
  seeded and chopped
¼ cup lemon juice
¼ cup olive oil
¾ cup cold water
2 cloves garlic, peeled and
  pressed
¼ cup chopped parsley
1 teaspoon salt
Fresh-ground pepper

In a large stainless steel or crockery mixing bowl, combine the ingredients, stirring to blend them well. Adjust the seasoning. Chill the gazpacho for at least 3 hours before serving it.

Avocado Mousse with Mixed Vegetable Salad

REFRIGERATES

PREPARATION: 30 MINUTES

CHILLING TIME: 3 HOURS FOR THE SALAD; 6 HOURS FOR THE MOUSSE

Egg whites may be substituted for the cream.

Two or three 10-ounce packages frozen mixed vegetables

In lightly salted boiling water to cover, cook the vegetables, uncovered, until they have just returned to the boil. Drain and refresh them in cold water. Drain them thoroughly.

Mayonnaise, page 252
Dijon mustard
¼ cup fine-chopped parsley
1 teaspoon dill weed

In a mixing bowl, combine the vegetables and sufficient mayonnaise to
bind them. Add mustard, to taste, and the parsley and dill weed. Fold
the mixture to blend it well. Chill the salad for at least 3 hours.

2 envelopes unflavored gelatin
⅓ cup lime juice
¾ teaspoon salt
1½ cups boiling water

In a mixing bowl, sprinkle the gelatin over the lime juice to soften. Add
the salt and then the boiling water, stirring to dissolve the gelatin.

1 very large or 2 small avocado, peeled, pitted, and chopped
  coarse
1 small onion, peeled and chopped coarse
4 tablespoons Mayonnaise, page 252
¾ teaspoon Worcestershire sauce

In the container of an electric blender, combine these four ingredients.
Over them, pour the gelatin water and, on medium speed, whirl the
mixture for 15 seconds, or until it is smooth.

3 ribs celery, diced fine

Return the mixture to the mixing bowl, stir in the celery, and chill until
it just begins to set.

1 cup heavy cream, whipped (or 4 egg whites, beaten until
  stiff but not dry with ½ teaspoon cream of tartar)

Into the avocado mixture, fold the whipped cream or egg white. Spoon
the mousse into a 1½-quart ring mold, rinsed with cold water, and chill
for at least 6 hours, or until it is set.

Salad Greens of your choice

To serve the dish, unmold the avocado ring on a bed of salad greens, fill
the center with some of the vegetable salad, and offer the remainder
separately.

Pineapple Flambé

DOUBLES / REFRIGERATES

PREPARATION: 15 MINUTES
CHILLING TIME: 1 HOUR

There is available a gadget which peels and cores pineapple in one opera-tion.

> 1 large ripe pineapple, the outer skin and eyes and inner
> core removed
> Sugar
> Kirschwasser

Cut the pineapple into 12 or 18 strips lengthwise, arrange them in a deep serving platter, sprinkle them with sugar and kirschwasser, to taste. Cover and chill the fruit.

> ⅓ cup cognac or orange-flavored liqueur

At the time of serving, heat the cognac or liqueur, ignite it, and pour it over the pineapple.

Onion Quiche
Mixed Salad, page 247
Cheeses of your choice, page 248
Strawberry Mousse

FOR 4 OR 6 PERSONS

A light *repas galant*. We tend to forget how good onions taste; this quiche celebrates their flavor. A mixed salad will do nicely to fill out the main part of the meal. Strawberry mousse is elegant and festive; if, however, you prefer something simpler to follow the quiche, Assorted Cheeses and Fresh Fruit, page 248, are always welcome.

Onion Quiche

PREPARATION: 25 MINUTES
COOKING: 30 MINUTES IN A 450°/325° F. OVEN

The preparation time does not include readying the pastry.

One 9-inch pastry shell, page 237

Prepare the pastry.

> 4 tablespoons butter
> 4 large onions, peeled and chopped

In a skillet, heat the butter and in it cook the onion until translucent.

> 3 eggs   1 teaspoon salt
> 2 cups light cream   ¼ teaspoon pepper
> ¼ teaspoon nutmeg

In a mixing bowl, beat the eggs lightly. Add the cream and seasonings; blend the mixture well.

At this point you may stop and continue later.

Over the bottom of the prepared pastry shell, arrange the onion in an even layer. Over the onion, pour the custard. Bake the quiche at 450° for 10 minutes; reduce the heat to 325° and continue to bake it for 20 minutes, or until the custard is set and the pastry is golden. Allow the quiche to stand for 5 minutes before cutting it.

Strawberry Mousse

REFRIGERATES

PREPARATION: 30 MINUTES
CHILLING TIME: 6 HOURS

The recipe may also be made with raspberries or ripe fresh peaches.

1 pint ripe strawberries, hulled, rinsed, and drained

Sieve the strawberries to yield 1 cup of pulp.

¼ cup sugar
1 envelope unflavored gelatin
Few grains of salt
½ cup hot water

In a saucepan, mix the sugar, gelatin, and salt. Add the water and heat the mixture, stirring constantly, to dissolve the sugar and gelatin.

Blend the fruit pulp with the gelatin. Chill the mixture until it is the consistency of egg white.

1 cup heavy cream, whipped

Into the fruit mixture, fold the whipped cream. Spoon it into a chilled 2-quart soufflé dish or serving bowl and refrigerate for at least 6 hours, or until the mousse is set.

Cream of Fresh Vegetable Soup
Mushroom Risotto
Beet Greens
Assorted Cheese and Fresh Fruit, page 248

FOR 6 PERSONS

Peas are the dominant vegetable in the soup—perhaps early peas from your garden. The risotto, from Italy, is light, subtle, and elegant. Beet greens, admittedly, are not elegant, but they are certainly a seasonal delight, available now at the greengrocer's. If you cannot find them, use spinach instead. Because the meal is simple, be a bit daring with the cheese and fruit—perhaps a Coulommiers and Bleu de Bresse and mangoes, if you can find them.

Cream of Fresh Vegetable Soup

DOUBLES / REFRIGERATES / FREEZES

PREPARATION: 50 MINUTES

The soup may be served hot or cold.

3 tablespoons butter
4 scallions, trimmed and chopped, with as much green as
    possible
3 tablespoons flour

In a large saucepan, heat the butter and in it cook the scallions until they are wilted. Stir in the flour and, over gentle heat, cook the mixture for a few minutes.

3 cups fresh peas (or two
    10-ounce packages
    frozen peas)
1 cup (packed) spinach leaves,
    the woody stems removed,
    thoroughly rinsed,
    and shredded

1 head Boston lettuce,
    rinsed and
    shredded
5 cups water
5 vegetable bouillon
    cubes
1 tablespoon sugar

To the contents of the saucepan, add these six ingredients. Bring the liquid to the boil, reduce the heat, and simmer the vegetables, covered, for 30 minutes, or until the peas are very tender.

In the container of an electric blender, whirl the mixture, on medium speed, two cups at a time, for 15 seconds, or until it is reduced to a smooth purée. Transfer the purée to a second saucepan.

1 cup heavy cream, scalded
Salt
Fresh-ground pepper

To the purée, add the cream, stirring to blend the soup well. Adjust the seasoning to taste.

Mushroom Risotto

DOUBLES / REFRIGERATES

PREPARATION: 15 MINUTES
COOKING: 50 MINUTES

¼ cup olive oil
1 clove garlic, peeled and split

In a skillet, heat the oil and in it cook the garlic until it is golden and the oil well flavored. Discard the garlic pieces.

1 pound mushrooms, sliced thin
¼ cup fine-chopped parsley
Salt
Fresh-ground pepper

In the oil, over moderate heat, cook the mushrooms and parsley, stirring, for 5 minutes, or until the mushrooms are tender. Season to taste, and reserve them.

3 tablespoons butter
1 medium onion, peeled and chopped
1½ cups brown rice

In a saucepan, heat the butter and in it cook the onion until translucent. Add the rice, stirring to coat each grain.

At this point you may stop and continue later.

2½ cups boiling water
½ cup dry white wine
3 vegetable bouillon cubes, powdered

To the rice, add the water, wine, and bouillon powder. Return the liquid to the boil, reduce the heat, and simmer the rice, covered, for 50 minutes, or until it is tender and the liquid is absorbed.

Meanwhile, over gentle heat, bring the mushrooms to serving temperature.

Grated Parmesan cheese

In a large, warmed serving bowl, lightly toss together the mushrooms and rice. Offer the cheese separately.

Beet Greens

DOUBLES

PREPARATION: 12 MINUTES
COOKING: 8 TO 10 MINUTES

Beet greens may be dressed simply with fresh lemon juice, with butter, with Oil-and-Lemon Dressing, page 256, or as is suggested for Spinach, Italian Style, page 204.

3 or 3½ quarts young beet greens, the woody stems removed, thoroughly washed in cold water, and drained
Salt
Fresh-ground pepper

In a soup kettle, arrange the beet greens; add a sprinkling of salt and pepper.

At this point you may stop and continue later.

Over high heat, bring the beet greens to the point of steaming; reduce the heat and simmer, covered, for 8 to 10 minutes, or until the stems are tender-crisp. Drain and dress the greens, as suggested above; reserve the essence for use in a soup.

Celeriac Rémoulade
French Potato Salad
Spinach with Sour Cream
Raspberry Mousse
Oatmeal Cookies, page 250

FOR 6 PERSONS

A pleasant supper for a warm spring evening. The potato salad, *garni*, is a surprisingly satisfying main dish, complemented by the less insistent flavor of the spinach. The meal, elegant and light, may be prepared well ahead of serving.

Celeriac Rémoulade

DOUBLES / REFRIGERATES

PREPARATION: 25 MINUTES
CHILLING TIME: 2 HOURS

This is the traditional French appetizer. A similar flavor may be captured, but not the texture, by cutting celery ribs into 2-inch julienne strips and tossing them with the rémoulade sauce.

2 medium bulbs celeriac
Boiling water

With a vegetable peeler, peel the celeriac. Using either a grater designed specifically for the purpose or a very sharp, heavy knife, grate or cut the celeriac into fine julienne strips. Arrange the vegetable in a mixing bowl and over it pour boiling water to cover; allow it to stand for 5 minutes. Drain and allow it to cool.

⅓ cup Mayonnaise,
    page 252
1 teaspoon Dijon mustard
2 tablespoons fine-chopped
    parsley
¼ teaspoon chervil

¼ teaspoon dried tarragon
    (or 1 teaspoon fresh,
    chopped fine)
Salt
Fresh-ground pepper

In a mixing bowl, combine and blend well the first five ingredients. To the sauce, add the celeriac and toss the mixture well. Adjust the seasoning to taste. Chill the celeriac, covered, until ready for use; it should be cool when served, but has more flavor if not taken directly from the refrigerator.

French Potato Salad

DOUBLES / REFRIGERATES

PREPARATION: 45 MINUTES
CHILLING TIME: 3 HOURS

6 medium potatoes, scrubbed

In boiling salted water to cover, cook the potatoes for 20 minutes, or until they are tender but still firm. Refresh them in cold water, peel, and cut them into medium-sized dice.

3 tablespoons white vinegar	1 teaspoon sugar
2 teaspoons Dijon-style mustard	¾ teaspoon salt
	¼ teaspoon white pepper
1 (or 2 or 3, to taste) cloves garlic, peeled and pressed	½ cup olive oil

In a jar with a tight-fitting lid, combine the vinegar, mustard, garlic, and seasonings. Shake the mixture vigorously to dissolve the sugar and salt. Add the olive oil and shake the dressing again to blend it well.

½ cup fine-chopped parsley

In a mixing bowl, combine the potatoes and parsley. Add the dressing and toss the salad well. Chill it, covered, for at least 3 hours.

Salad greens
6 hard-boiled eggs, peeled and halved
3 ripe tomatoes, peeled and cut in wedges

At the time of serving the salad, arrange it on a bed of greens and garnish it with the eggs and tomato wedges.

Spinach with Sour Cream

DOUBLES / REFRIGERATES

PREPARATION: 30 MINUTES
COOKING: 15 MINUTES IN A 300° F. OVEN

If desired, ½ cup grated Parmesan cheese may be added when you blend the spinach and sour cream.

Three 10-ounce packages fresh spinach, the woody stems removed, rinsed in cold water (or three 10-ounce packages frozen chopped spinach, fully thawed to room
temperature)

In a soup kettle, arrange the fresh spinach with only the water that
clings to it. Over high heat, cook the spinach until steam rises; reduce
the heat to medium, cover, and continue to cook until it is just wilted
(about 30 seconds). Drain and press it dry in a colander. Chop it. (If
you use frozen chopped spinach, you need not cook it unless you wish
to do so—I never do. Drain and press it dry in a colander.)

Sour cream
Salt
Fresh-ground pepper

In a mixing bowl, blend the prepared spinach with sour cream to taste.
The mixture should not be liquid. Season it to taste.
    Transfer the spinach to an oven-proof serving dish.

At this point you may stop and continue later.

Heat the spinach, covered, in a 300° oven for 15 minutes, or until it
reaches the desired temperature.

Raspberry Mousse

DOUBLES / REFRIGERATES

PREPARATION: 20 MINUTES
CHILLING TIME: 6 HOURS

1 envelope unflavored gelatin softened in ½ cup cold water

Over hot water, dissolve the gelatin.
    Wrap a 1½-quart soufflé dish with a 3-inch collar of foil, lightly oiled;
or, if you prefer, use a 2-quart soufflé dish, or other serving bowl without
the collar. Chill the utensil.

Two 10-ounce packages frozen raspberries, fully thawed to
room temperature

Sieve the raspberries and discard the seeds. In a mixing bowl, combine
and blend the gelatin and raspberry purée.

¼ teaspoon lemon extract
3 tablespoons sugar
Few grains of salt

Add the lemon extract, sugar, and salt, stirring until the sugar is dissolved. Chill the mixture until it is the consistency of egg white.

1 cup heavy cream
¼ cup sugar

Whip the heavy cream, gradually adding the sugar, until the cream is stiff. Fold it into the raspberry purée.

Spoon the mixture into the prepared dish, and chill for at least 6 hours.

Menus for Summer

Vichyssoise
Eggplant and Rice en Casserole
Summer Squash
Blueberries with Honey

A French soup, a Middle Eastern main dish, and a vegetable and dessert from America—the combination of nationalities recalls my university days when students from all over the world congregated at International House for relaxation and a shared meal.

Vichyssoise

DOUBLES / REFRIGERATES / FREEZES

PREPARATION: 1 HOUR
CHILLING TIME: 3 HOURS

> 2 tablespoons butter
> 4 leeks, trimmed, rinsed, and chopped (the white part only)
> 1 medium onion, peeled and chopped

In a large saucepan, heat the butter and in it, over moderate heat, cook the leek and onion until golden.

> 5 medium potatoes, peeled
>   and chopped coarse
> 4 cups water

> 4 vegetable bouillon cubes
> 1 teaspoon salt
> ½ teaspoon white pepper

75

Add the potato, water, bouillon cubes, and seasonings. Boil, covered, for
30 minutes, or until the potato is very tender.

In the container of an electric blender, whirl the mixture on medium
speed, 2 cups at a time, until it is reduced to a smooth purée. Transfer
the purée to a serving bowl.

> 2 cups milk
> 2 cups heavy cream
> Chopped chives

In the saucepan, combine the milk and cream and scald the mixture.
Add it to the purée, stirring to blend the vichyssoise well. Adjust the
seasoning to taste. Chill the soup for at least 3 hours. Serve it garnished
with the chives.

Eggplant and Rice en Casserole

DOUBLES / REFRIGERATES / FREEZES

PREPARATION: 1 HOUR
COOKING: 20 MINUTES IN A 400° F. OVEN

> ¼ cup olive oil   2½ cups water
> 2 onions, peeled and   ½ teaspoon basil
>   chopped   1 teaspoon salt
> One 6-ounce can tomato   Fresh-ground pepper
>   paste

Heat the oil and, in it, cook the onion until it is translucent. Stir in the
tomato paste, water, and seasonings. Simmer the mixture, uncovered,
for 30 minutes.

> 1¼ cups water
> 2 vegetable bouillon cubes

To the sauce, add the water and bouillon cubes; simmer the mixture,
covered, for 15 minutes. While the sauce is simmering, cook the eggplant.

> Olive oil
> 1 large eggplant, peeled and cut in ¼-inch slices

In a skillet, heat olive oil as needed and, over high heat, quickly brown the eggplant slices on both sides; as they are done, remove them to absorbent paper.

> **4 tablespoons butter, softened**
> **Salt**
> **Fresh-ground pepper**

When the tomato sauce has simmered, stir in the butter. Adjust the seasoning to taste.

> **1 cup raw white rice**
> **¼ pound mozzarella cheese, sliced**
> **¼ cup grated Parmesan cheese**

Into a casserole or baking dish, spoon one-third of the tomato sauce. Add one-half of the rice, then one-half of the eggplant; over the egg-plant, arrange a layer of one-half of the mozzarella. Repeat the layers, beginning again with the sauce. End with the final third of the sauce, and, over it, sprinkle the Parmesan cheese.

At this point you may stop and continue later.

Bake the casserole at 400° for 20 minutes, or until the rice is tender and most of the liquid is absorbed.

Summer Squash

DOUBLES

PREPARATION: 10 MINUTES
COOKING: 10 MINUTES

> **2 tablespoons butter**   **Cumin**
> **4 or 5 small summer (yellow)**   **Salt**
> ** squash, the ends trimmed,**   **Fresh-ground pepper**
> ** and sliced thin**

In a skillet with a cover, heat the butter. To it, add the squash and a sprinkling of cumin, salt, and pepper. Over high heat, shake the pan, or stir, to coat the squash.

At this point you may stop and continue later.

Fine-chopped parsley

Over high heat, bring the squash to steaming temperature; reduce the heat and simmer it, covered, for 10 minutes, or until it is tender but still holds its shape. Serve it garnished with a sprinkling of chopped parsley.

Blueberries with Honey

DOUBLES / REFRIGERATES

PREPARATION: 15 MINUTES

CHILLING TIME: 2 HOURS

> 2 pints blueberries, picked over, rinsed, and drained in a
>   colander
> ¼ cup honey

In a mixing bowl, combine the blueberries and honey and gently toss the berries until they are evenly coated. Transfer the berries to a serving dish and chill them for 2 hours.

Cream of Carrot Soup
Greek Salad
Lima Beans in Lemon Sauce (optional)
Muffins, page 235
Peach Tart with Crumb Topping

FOR 6 PERSONS

If one had an obliging peach tree (alas, I do not), one might produce the better part of this meal from one's garden. Still, I *have* managed the soup, the vegetable ingredients of the salad, and the lima beans from my vegetable patch—with gratifying pleasure. If you are garden-less, however, hurry to your greengrocer's, for the combination is unusual, easily prepared, and attractive to look at.

Cream of Carrot Soup

DOUBLES / REFRIGERATES / FREEZES

PREPARATION: 1¼ HOURS

    4 tablespoons butter
    6 medium large carrots, scraped and sliced
    1 medium potato, peeled and chopped
    2 medium onions, peeled and chopped

In a large saucepan, heat the butter and in it, over moderate heat, cook
the vegetables, covered, for 15 minutes.

    4 cups water
    4 vegetable bouillon cubes
    1 bay leaf

To the vegetables, add these three ingredients and simmer the mixture,
covered, for 45 minutes, or until the carrots are very tender. Remove the
bay leaf.

    In the container of an electric blender, whirl the mixture on medium
speed, 2 cups at a time, for 15 seconds, or until it is reduced to a smooth
purée.

    2 cups milk, scalded
    Salt
    Fresh-ground white pepper
    Fine-chopped parsley

To the purée, add the milk, stirring to blend the soup well. Adjust the
seasoning to taste. Serve the soup hot, garnished with a sprinkling of
parsley.

Greek Salad

DOUBLES / REFRIGERATES (COVER CLOSELY WITH PLASTIC WRAP)

PREPARATION: 25 MINUTES

*In Greece, the salad is not offered in individual portions, but is arranged
on a large platter and placed in the center of the table so that each person helps himself.*

1 large head Boston lettuce, rinsed and the leaves dried

On a large serving plate, arrange a bed of the lettuce leaves.

1 large cucumber, peeled and sliced	1 cup ripe olives (pitted or oil-cured
3 large ripe tomatoes, peeled and sliced	1½ pounds feta cheese, cut in 12 pieces
1 large red or Bermuda onion, peeled and sliced	Oregano Juice of 1 large lemon
1 green pepper, seeded and cut in julienne strips	Olive oil Salt
2 young zucchini, trimmed and sliced	Fresh-ground pepper

Over the lettuce, in an attractive pattern, arrange the first seven ingredients. Sprinkle the salad with oregano, the lemon juice, olive oil, salt, and pepper to taste.

6 hard-cooked eggs, peeled and halved

Add the eggs just before serving.

Lima Beans in Lemon Sauce

DOUBLES / REFRIGERATES / FREEZES

PREPARATION: 30 MINUTES

The preparation time does not include shelling the beans.

½ cup salted water	Salt
4 tablespoons butter	Fresh-ground pepper
½ teaspoon rosemary, crumbled	
4½ pounds (1½ pounds shelled) lima beans (or two 10-ounce packages frozen lima beans)	

In a saucepan, bring the water to a boil. Add the butter and rosemary and, when the butter is melted, add the beans, stirring to coat them well. Cook the beans, covered, over moderately high heat, for 20 minutes, or until they are tender. Season them to taste.

Grated rind and juice of 1 medium lemon
1 teaspoon cornstarch

In a cup or small bowl, combine the lemon rind, juice, and cornstarch. Stir the mixture until it is smooth.

Fine-chopped parsley

Add the cornstarch to the beans, stirring constantly until the sauce is thickened and smooth. Serve the lima beans garnished with a sprinkling of parsley.

Peach Tart with Crumb Topping

Follow the directions for Fresh Pineapple Tart, page 156, using, in place of the pineapple, 2½ pounds firm ripe peaches, peeled and sliced.

Mushrooms Chantilly, page 46
Stuffed Peppers, Italian Style
Purée of Lima Beans with Horseradish
Peach Charlotte

FOR 6 PERSONS

I especially enjoy this main dish, which I find subtler in flavor than most recipes for stuffed peppers. The Peach Charlotte is attractively festive. A pleasant meal, partially derived from your garden, if you wish, and, what to me is more important, uncomplicated in its preparation.

Stuffed Peppers, Italian Style

DOUBLES

PREPARATION: 20 MINUTES

COOKING: 40 MINUTES IN A 350° F. OVEN

The preparation time does not include readying the tomato sauce.

6 green peppers

In boiling water to cover, cook the peppers for 5 minutes. Drain and refresh them in cold water. Cut off the stem ends and seed them.

One 1-pound can tomatoes, drained and chopped
4 cups croutons
12 pitted ripe olives, drained and sliced
⅓ cup grated Parmesan cheese
¼ cup fine-chopped parsley
1 clove garlic, chopped fine
¾ teaspoon salt
Fresh-ground pepper, to taste

In a mixing bowl, combine and toss together these eight ingredients. Stuff the peppers with the mixture, stand them in an oven-proof serving dish and cover until ready to cook them.

At this point you may stop and continue later.

Tomato Sauce, page 253

Bake the peppers, uncovered, at 350° for 40 minutes. Serve them, if desired, accompanied by tomato sauce.

Purée of Lima Beans with Horseradish

DOUBLES / REFRIGERATES / FREEZES

PREPARATION: 35 MINUTES

This recipe may be fully prepared in advance and reheated at the time of serving.

4½ pounds (1½ pounds shelled) lima beans (or two or three 10-ounce packages frozen lima beans)

In boiling salted water to cover, cook the beans, covered, for 25 minutes, or until they are tender. Drain them well.

½ cup heavy cream
2 tablespoons soft butter
1½ tablespoons prepared
    horseradish (or to taste)

Salt
Fresh-ground pepper

To the beans, add the cream, butter, and horseradish. In the container of an electric blender, whirl the mixture on medium speed until it is reduced to a smooth purée. Season it to taste.

Peach Charlotte

REFRIGERATES / FREEZES

PREPARATION: 25 MINUTES
CHILLING TIME: 6 HOURS

The dessert may be made with canned peaches, thoroughly drained and chopped coarse.

1 envelope unflavored gelatin softened in ¼ cup cold water.

Over simmering water, dissolve the gelatin. Allow it to cool.

Lady fingers (about 18)
Sweet sherry

Line a charlotte mold or 1½-quart soufflé dish with lady fingers and sprinkle them with sherry.

1 cup heavy cream
½ cup confectioners' sugar

In a mixing bowl, combine the cream and sugar and whip the mixture until it is firm. Reserve it.

1½ pounds ripe peaches, peeled, seeded, and chopped coarse
Prepared gelatin
Reserved whipped cream

In a large mixing bowl, combine the peaches and gelatin. Into them, fold the whipped cream. Pour the mixture into the prepared mold and chill the dessert for at least 6 hours, or until it is set.

Spinach Soup
Casserole of Mixed Vegetables
Muffins (optional), page 235
Compote of Peaches and Pears

FOR 4 PERSONS

A very easy menu. So easy, in fact, that the main dish has no "stop-and-continue-later" point. If you wish, however, you may ready all the ingredients for the casserole and cook them rapidly at the time of serving.

Spinach Soup

DOUBLES / REFRIGERATES / FREEZES

PREPARATION: 25 MINUTES

A Norwegian favorite which may be served hot or chilled.

2 tablespoons butter	One 10-ounce package fresh
4 tablespoons flour	spinach, rinsed (or one
6 cups water	10-ounce package frozen
4 vegetable bouillon	chopped spinach fully
cubes	thawed to room temperature)

In a large saucepan, heat the butter and in it cook the flour, stirring, until it is golden. Add the water, stirring to keep the mixture smooth. Add the bouillon cubes and spinach. Bring the soup to the boil and cook it, covered, for 10 minutes.

In the container of an electric blender, whirl the mixture on medium speed, two cups at a time, until the spinach is chopped fine. Transfer the soup to a serving bowl. (If you use frozen spinach, omit this step.)

1 cup heavy cream, scalded
Grating of nutmeg
Salt
Fresh-ground pepper

Add the cream. Season the soup with a generous grating of nutmeg and salt and pepper to taste.

Casserole of Mixed Vegetables

DOUBLES

PREPARATION: 15 MINUTES
COOKING: 15 MINUTES

This simple but exquisite recipe is contributed by my country neighbor, Ellen Fagergren.

3 tablespoons butter
2 tablespoons olive oil
1 large onion, peeled and
   chopped coarse
1 large zucchini, trimmed
   and cut in ¼-inch rounds
1 medium cucumber, peeled
   and chopped

1 small eggplant, peeled and
   chopped coarse
1 large ripe tomato,
   peeled, seeded and
   chopped
Salt
Fresh-ground pepper

In a flame-proof casserole, heat the butter and oil and in it sauté the five vegetables. Cover and simmer them for 10 minutes; remove the cover and continue simmering them for 5 minutes to evaporate the excess moisture. Add salt and pepper to taste.

Compote of Peaches and Pears

DOUBLES / REFRIGERATES

PREPARATION: 15 MINUTES
CHILLING TIME: 2 HOURS

3 or 4 large ripe peaches,
   peeled, pitted, and sliced
3 or 4 firm ripe pears, peeled,
   cored, and sliced

Juice of 1 lemon,
   sieved
½ cup sugar
Chopped fresh mint

In a serving bowl, gently toss the fruit with the lemon juice. Add the sugar and once again toss the mixture to blend it. Chill the compote for at least 2 hours before serving it, garnished with a light sprinkling of mint.

Parsley and Lettuce Soup
Fresh Tomatoes with Pesto
         or
Ring Mold of Green Peas
Muffins, page 235
Compote of Peaches with Honey
Oatmeal Cookies (optional), page 250

FOR 4 PERSONS

Pesto, or *pesto genovese*, that superb sauce of fresh basil which we in this country know largely as an accompaniment to pasta (a superb dish and one which you should try!) and occasionally as an adornment to minestrone, is here used for the delight which is its own. I know city-dwelling people who grow basil on their window sills in order to enjoy *pesto* during the summer season. If you are unable to find fresh basil, offer instead the ring mold of green peas, also a delightful summer dish.

Parsley and Lettuce Soup

Follow the directions for Watercress Soup, page 117, using, in place of the watercress, 1 very large bunch of parsley, the heavy stems removed.

Fresh Tomatoes with Pesto

PREPARATION: 20 MINUTES

To double the recipe, make the sauce twice. The sauce refrigerates and freezes; when frozen, allow it to thaw fully to room temperature before homogenizing by stirring it vigorously.

2 cloves garlic, peeled	2 tablespoons pine nuts (pignoli)
½ cup olive oil	4 tablespoons grated Parmesan
¼ cup water	cheese
2 tablespoons soft butter	Pinch of salt

In the container of an electric blender, combine these eight ingredients and, on medium speed, whirl them until the mixture is smootn.

1 cup (packed) fresh basil leaves (dried basil will not do)

To the contents of the blender, running at medium speed, add the basil leaves, a few at a time. (More olive oil may be added, if necessary, to facilitate blending the basil with the other ingredients.)

Transfer the sauce to a bowl and press plastic wrap onto the surface (exposed to air, *pesto* darkens). Use the sauce at room temperature.

4 large ripe tomatoes, peeled
Salad greens

Cut off the stem ends of the tomatoes and remove a little of the pulp. Cover and chill the tomatoes. Prepare salad greens of your choice.

At this point you may stop and continue later.

Fill the cavity of each tomato with some of the *pesto*. Serve them on a bed of salad greens.

Ring Mold of Green Peas

PREPARATION: 20 MINUTES

COOKING: 30 MINUTES IN A 350° F. OVEN

Three 10-ounce packages
    frozen green peas, cooked
    until very tender in lightly
    salted boiling water to
    cover, drained
4 tablespoons melted butter

¼ cup light cream
1 medium onion, peeled and
    chopped coarse
3 egg yolks
Salt
Fresh-ground pepper

In the container of an electric blender, combine the peas, butter, cream, and onion. On medium speed, whirl the mixture until it is reduced to a smooth purée. Add the egg yolks and blend the mixture again. Season it to taste.

At this point you may stop and continue later.

3 egg whites, beaten until stiff but not dry

Into a mixing bowl, pour the purée. Fold a little of it into the egg white; then fold all of the egg white back into the purée.

    Pour the mixture into a buttered 1½-quart ring mold. Place the mold in a pan of hot water. Bake the dish at 350° for 30 minutes, or until it is well puffed. Unmold the ring onto a heated serving dish and garnish with Carrots Vichy (page 47).

Compote of Peaches with Honey

DOUBLES / REFRIGERATES

PREPARATION: 15 MINUTES

CHILLING TIME: 2 HOURS

6 large ripe peaches, peeled
Juice of 1 medium lemon, sieved
⅓ cup honey

Into a serving bowl, slice the peaches. Add the lemon juice and gently toss the fruit to prevent its darkening. Add the honey and gently toss the compote once again. Chill the compote for at least 2 hours.

Baked Mushroom Canapés, page 31
Ratatouille
Muffins, page 235
Fresh Fruit Mousse
Oatmeal Cookies (optional), page 250

FOR 6 PERSONS

Ratatouille, a savory Mediterranean vegetable casserole, is the central focus of this menu, in a recipe I acquired from friends in France. Ratatouille should be moist, but not watery; slow cooking helps to assure the preferred consistency. It may be served chilled, at room temperature, or hot; my favorite way is hot, even in very warm weather, but it is also pleasant at room temperature, especially when accompanied, as it is here, by hot bread. Following upon the strong-flavored ratatouille, the mousse is cool and refreshingly light.

Ratatouille

DOUBLES / REFRIGERATES

PREPARATION: 30 MINUTES
COOKING: 1¼ HOURS

There is no point at which you can logically stop and continue later. Either prepare the ratatouille completely and reheat it at the time of serving (my way) or ready the ingredients in advance and cook it just before serving.

¼ cup olive oil
2 large onions, peeled and sliced
2 or 3 cloves garlic, peeled and chopped

In a flame-proof casserole, heat the olive oil and in it cook the onion and garlic until the onion is barely golden.

> 1 medium-large eggplant, cut into 1-inch cubes and dredged
>   in seasoned flour (page 238)
> 1 large green pepper, seeded and cut into julienne strips

To the onion, add the eggplant and pepper. Over gentle heat, simmer the vegetables, covered, for 1 hour, stirring them often.

> 3 medium zucchini, trimmed   1 teaspoon oregano
>   and sliced   1½ teaspoons sugar
> 4 medium ripe tomatoes, peeled,   Salt
>   seeded, chopped, and drained   Fresh-ground pepper

To the simmering casserole, add the zucchini, tomatoes, oregano, and sugar. Stir the vegetables gently to blend the mixture well. Continue to cook the ratatouille, uncovered, stirring it often, for 15 minutes, or until the zucchini are just tender and the dish is of the moisture you prefer. Adjust the seasoning with salt and pepper to taste.

Fresh Fruit Mousse

REFRIGERATES

PREPARATION: 30 MINUTES
MACERATION TIME: 3 HOURS
CHILLING TIME: 6 HOURS

> 1 cup honey dew balls   2 tablespoons
> 1 cup cantaloupe balls   superfine
> 1 cup seedless grapes, stemmed,   sugar
>   rinsed, and dried on   ½ cup light rum
>   absorbent paper

In a mixing bowl, combine the fruits, sprinkle them with the sugar and pour the rum over them. Allow the mixture to macerate, refrigerated, for 3 hours.

> 1½ envelopes unflavored gelatin
> ¼ cup light rum

Soften the gelatin in the rum.

4 egg yolks

⅔ cup sugar, mixed with ½ teaspoon cornstarch and a few
grains of salt

1½ cups milk

In the top of a double boiler, lightly beat the egg yolks. Add the remaining ingredients and, over gently boiling water, cook the mixture,
stirring constantly, until it thickens and coats the spoon. Add the gelatin, stirring to dissolve it. Allow the custard to cool.

4 egg whites, beaten until stiff

Drain the fruit of any excess liquid. Fold the fruit into the custard and
then fold in the egg whites. Spoon the mixture into a lightly oiled
2-quart soufflé dish or mold. Chill the mousse for at least 6 hours, or
until it is set.

Green Bean Soup
Cabbage Rolls
Fresh Lima Beans
Salad (optional), page 245
Cold Lime Soufflé

FOR 6 PERSONS

Another dinner from your garden—save for the soufflé. The soup and
main dish are unusual and tasty. Offer a big salad of tender greens and
arugola. The dessert is cool and decorative.

Green Bean Soup

DOUBLES / REFRIGERATES / FREEZES

PREPARATION: 1 HOUR

5 cups water
5 vegetable bouillon cubes
1 pound young green beans,
    rinsed and chopped coarse
1 medium potato, peeled
    and cubed

1 medium onion,
    peeled and
    quartered
½ teaspoon salt
¼ teaspoon pepper

In a soup kettle or large saucepan, combine these seven ingredients. Bring the water to the boil, reduce the heat, and simmer, covered, for 40 minutes, or until the vegetables are very tender.

In the container of an electric blender, whirl the mixture on medium speed, 2 cups at a time, until it is reduced to a smooth purée. Transfer the purée to a second saucepan.

1 cup heavy cream, scalded
Worcestershire sauce
Salt
Butter-toasted croutons (optional)

To the purée, add the cream, stirring to blend the soup well. Season it to taste with a little Worcestershire sauce and, if needed, additional salt. Serve the soup hot or cold, garnished, if desired, with a sprinkling of croutons.

Cabbage Rolls

DOUBLES / REFRIGERATES / FREEZES

PREPARATION: 40 MINUTES
COOKING: 1½ HOURS IN A 350° F. OVEN

12 large cabbage leaves, the woody base removed

In boiling water to cover, parboil the cabbage leaves for 3 minutes. Refresh them in cold water; drain and dry them.

1 cup raw white rice
2 cups water

In a saucepan, combine the rice and water; bring the liquid to the
boil, reduce the heat, and simmer the rice, covered, for 15 minutes, or
until it is tender and the liquid is absorbed.

2 onions, peeled and chopped fine	¼ teaspoon pepper
⅓ cup chopped parsley	½ cup Fontina cheese, shredded
Grating of nutmeg	½ cup Provolone cheese, shredded
¼ teaspoon sage	
1½ teaspoons salt	

To the rice, add these eight ingredients. Blend them well.

On each of the cabbage leaves, spoon an equal quantity of the rice
mixture. Form rolls by folding the sides of the leaves over and then
rolling the leaf closed. In a lightly oiled baking dish, arrange the rolls
in a single layer with the folded side down.

*At this point you may stop and continue later. (Also, at this point you
may freeze the dish to cook at your convenience.)*

One 29-ounce can Italian tomatoes

Over the cabbage rolls, pour the tomatoes. Bake at 350° for 1½ hours.

Fresh Lima Beans

DOUBLES / REFRIGERATES

PREPARATION: 35 MINUTES
COOKING: 20 MINUTES

4½ pounds lima beans

Shell the beans. You should have 1½ pounds shelled limas to serve six
persons.

In boiling salted water to cover, cook the beans, covered, for 15 to 20
minutes, or until they are tender. Drain and arrange them in a heated
serving dish.

Soft butter
Salt
Fresh-ground pepper

Dress the beans with butter and season them with salt and pepper to taste.

Cold Lime Soufflé

Follow the directions for Cold Lemon Soufflé, page 30, using, in place of the lemon, an equal quantity of lime juice and rind; increase the sugar to ¾ cup. Add a few drops of green food coloring.

Gazpacho, page 60
Corn and Cheese Soufflé
Green Beans with Water Chestnuts
Compote of Blueberries and Strawberries

FOR 4 PERSONS

A menu from Mexico, America, and China which uses foods from your garden and seasonal blueberries, readily available at your market. Prepare the gazpacho well in advance so that the flavors meld. If you ready the ingredients for the main and side dishes in advance, the meal will be produced with a minimum of effort and a maximum of time spent with family or friends.

Corn and Cheese Soufflé

PREPARATION: 25 MINUTES
COOKING: 30 MINUTES IN A 350° F. OVEN

All ingredients for the soufflé and its dish may be readied in advance.

2 cups fresh corn, scraped from the cob (about 6 medium ears)

Prepare the corn.

4 tablespoons butter	¼ cup grated Gruyère
4 tablespoons flour	cheese
¼ teaspoon paprika	¼ cup grated Parmesan
1¼ teaspoons salt	cheese
¼ teaspoon pepper	4 egg yolks
¾ cup milk	Prepared corn

In a saucepan, heat the butter and in it, over gentle heat, cook the flour for a few minutes. Stir in the seasonings. Gradually add the milk, stirring constantly until the mixture is thickened and smooth. Add the cheeses, stirring to melt them. Beat in the egg yolks. Finally, add the prepared corn and blend the mixture well.

4 egg whites, beaten until stiff but not dry

Fold the egg whites into the corn mixture. Spoon the batter into a lightly buttered 2-quart soufflé dish. Bake at 350° for 30 minutes, or until the soufflé is well puffed and golden. Serve it at once.

Green Beans with Water Chestnuts

DOUBLES

PREPARATION: 20 MINUTES

A dish in the Chinese style best made by preparing the ingredients in advance and cooking them quickly at the time of serving.

3 tablespoons oil
1 pound green beans, the stem ends trimmed, cut diagonally in 2-inch pieces
12 scallions, trimmed and cut diagonally in ½-inch pieces (omit the green part)

In a wok or casserole, heat the oil and in it, over high heat, stir-fry the beans for 4 minutes. Add the scallions and continue to cook the vegetables for 3 minutes.

¼ cup water
1 vegetable bouillon cube, crumbled to a powder

To the vegetables, add the water and bouillon powder. Reduce the heat and simmer the vegetables, covered, for 4 minutes.

One 8-ounce can water chestnuts, drained and sliced

Add the water chestnuts and heat them through.

Compote of Blueberries and Strawberries

DOUBLES / REFRIGERATES

PREPARATION: 15 MINUTES
CHILLING TIME: 2 HOURS

1 pint blueberries, rinsed, picked over, and drained
1 pint strawberries, hulled, rinsed, drained, and halved
Brandy-and-Honey Sauce, page 258

In a serving bowl, combine the berries and gently toss with enough sauce to coat them. Chill the dessert for at least 2 hours.

Fresh Tomato Soup
Potato Salad with Sour Cream and Dill
Braised Cucumbers
Cold Lemon Soufflé, page 30

FOR 6 PERSONS

A cold meal, excepting the cucumber, designed for a hot day when the kitchen range is less than inviting—hence the "stop-and-continue-later"

point in cooking the very simple cucumber recipe. A seasonal menu
which you may garner from your garden or supermarket and prepare
with cool assurance that it will be popular.

Fresh Tomato Soup

DOUBLES / REFRIGERATES / FREEZES

PREPARATION TIME: 1 HOUR

3 pounds fresh ripe tomatoes, quartered	6 ribs celery, chopped, with leaves
4 medium carrots, scrubbed and chopped	1 bunch parsley
1 large onion, peeled and chopped	6 sprigs fresh mint or 1 tablespoon dried mint
	4 bay leaves

In a soup kettle, combine these seven ingredients and, over medium
heat, cook them, covered, for 40 minutes, or until the carrots are very
tender (the tomatoes will make adequate liquid).

Remove and discard the bay leaves. In the container of an electric
blender, whirl the mixture, about two cups at a time, for 15 seconds, or
until the purée is smooth. Put it into a second kettle or large saucepan.

6 tablespoons butter

To the purée, add the butter and, over gentle heat, cook the mixture,
stirring, until the butter is melted.

2 cups light cream, scalded	Sugar
1 cup heavy cream (optional), scalded	Salt
2 cups milk, scalded	Fresh-ground pepper

Stir in the light cream and, if a richer soup is desired, the heavy cream.
Finally, stir in the milk, to taste. Season the soup, to taste.

Croutons toasted in garlic butter
Chopped chives, mint, or parsley

If the soup has been frozen, thaw it fully, whirl it in the container of an
electric blender, and, if it is to be served cold, chill it; or heat to serving

temperature. Stir the soup well before serving it. If desired, select a garnish of your choice.

Potato Salad with Sour Cream and Dill

DOUBLES / REFRIGERATES

PREPARATION: 30 MINUTES
CHILLING TIME: 2 HOURS

>   6 medium potatoes, scrubbed

In boiling water to cover, cook the potatoes for 20 minutes, or until they
are fork-tender but still firm. Refresh them in cold water; peel and dice
them.

3 ribs celery, sliced	4 tablespoons vinegar
6 scallions, sliced thin	1 cup sour cream
(the white part only)	3 or 4 sprigs dill, chopped (or
½ green pepper, seeded	1½ teaspoons dried dill)
and chopped	1 teaspoon salt
½ sweet red pepper, seeded	Fresh-ground pepper
and chopped (optional)	

In a large mixing bowl, combine the potato with the remaining ingredients. Gently toss the mixture to blend it thoroughly. Chill the salad
for 2 hours.

>   Salad greens
>   Tomato wedges
>   Hard-cooked eggs (optional)

Serve the potato salad on greens of your choice, garnished with tomato
wedges and, if desired, hard-cooked eggs, halved.

Braised Cucumbers

DOUBLES

PREPARATION: 12 MINUTES
COOKING: 5 MINUTES

>   3 tablespoons butter
>   6 medium cucumbers, peeled, halved both length- and cross-
>   wise, and seeded

In a skillet or flame-proof serving dish, heat the butter and in it sauté the cucumbers on both sides until they are lightly golden.

¼ cup water
1 vegetable bouillon cube, powdered

Combine the water and bouillon powder and pour the liquid over the cucumbers.

At this point you may stop and continue later.

Dried dill weed
Salt
Fresh-ground pepper

Over gentle heat, cook the cucumbers for 5 minutes, or until they are tender-crisp. Sprinkle them with dill weed. Adjust the seasoning to taste.

Cream of Asparagus Soup
Jellied Broccoli Ring
Carrots and Peas in Curried Mayonnaise
Muffins, page 235
Fresh Fruit Compote
Oatmeal Cookies, page 250

FOR 6 PERSONS

A summer (or late spring) menu which allows vegetable gardeners to show off a bit. There is a quality of freshness about these dishes, and, for this reason, I urge a trip to your greengrocer or supermarket for any produce your backyard does not provide. Home-made asparagus soup tastes nothing like commercial varieties. Fill the broccoli ring with some of the carrots and peas and serve those remaining in a separate dish.

Once again, you will notice that the greater part of the dinner is prepared well beforehand, leaving you free to enjoy a pleasant afternoon.

Cream of Asparagus Soup

DOUBLES / REFRIGERATES / FREEZES

PREPARATION: 1 HOUR

1 pound asparagus stalks, saved from occasions when you have served asparagus, cut into 1-inch pieces split lengthwise	3 cups hot water
	4 vegetable bouillon cubes
	1 cup dry white wine
2 medium onions, peeled and chopped coarse	½ teaspoon mace
	¼ teaspoon white pepper

In a large saucepan, combine these seven ingredients. Bring the liquid to the boil, reduce the heat, and simmer, covered, for 30 minutes.

In the container of an electric blender, whirl the soup on medium speed, 2 cups at a time, until it is reduced to a smooth purée. Sieve it into a saucepan.

   3 tablespoons butter
   3 tablespoons flour

In a small saucepan, heat the butter and in it cook the flour for a few minutes. Add the *roux* to the soup and bring it to the boil, stirring constantly until it is somewhat thickened and smooth.

   1 cup heavy cream, scalded
   Juice of ½ small lemon
   Salt

Stir in the cream and lemon juice and adjust the seasoning, to taste.

The soup may be served hot or cold (I prefer it hot). If served hot, butter-toasted croutons make a nice garnish; if cold, use chopped chives or parsley or a suggestion of chopped fresh mint.

Jellied Broccoli Ring

REFRIGERATES

PREPARATION: 30 MINUTES
CHILLING TIME: 6 HOURS

3 cups hot water
3 vegetable bouillon cubes
2 large heads broccoli, the large stems
    peeled and split (or two 10-ounce
    packages frozen chopped broccoli)

1 onion, peeled and
    chopped

In a large saucepan, combine the water, bouillon cubes, broccoli, and onion. Bring the liquid to the boil and cook the broccoli, covered, for 12 minutes, or until it is tender-crisp. Remove the broccoli from the saucepan, reserving the water, and chop it. Return it to the cooking liquid in the saucepan. (Cook frozen chopped broccoli according to the directions on the package; do not remove it from the cooking liquid.)

2 envelopes unflavored gelatin, softened in ¼ cup cold
    water
Grated rind and juice of 1 lemon

To the broccoli, add the gelatin, lemon rind, and juice, stirring until the gelatin is dissolved.

½ cup Mayonnaise, page 252
½ cup chopped celery
⅓ cup chopped parsley

Sugar
Tabasco sauce
Salt

Add the first three ingredients, stirring to blend the mixture well; adjust the seasoning to taste with a little sugar, a few drops of Tabasco, and salt. Pour the mixture into a 1½-quart ring mold rinsed with cold water. Chill for at least 6 hours, or until set.

At the time of serving, unmold the ring onto a large, chilled serving platter and fill the center with some of the Carrots and Peas in Curried Mayonnaise.

Carrots and Peas in Curried Mayonnaise

DOUBLES / REFRIGERATES

PREPARATION: 45 MINUTES
CHILLING TIME: 2 HOURS

The recipe may be prepared with three 10-ounce packages frozen carrots and peas (or, if desired, three 10-ounce packages of frozen mixed vegetables), cooked according to the directions on the package; do not overcook the vegetables.

1½ cups scraped, thin-sliced carrots
1½ cups green peas

In boiling salted water to cover, cook the carrots for 6 minutes; add the peas and continue to cook the vegetables 5 minutes longer, or until they are tender-crisp. Refresh them in cold water; drain them thoroughly.

½ cup Curried Mayonnaise, page 253

In a mixing bowl, combine the carrots, peas, and sufficient mayonnaise to bind the vegetables. Using two forks, gently toss the mixture to blend it well. Chill the carrots and peas for at least 2 hours.

Fresh Fruit Compote

DOUBLES / REFRIGERATES

PREPARATION: 30 MINUTES
CHILLING TIME: 3 HOURS

Poaching Syrup for Fruit Compotes, page 259

Prepare the syrup.

3 large firm ripe peaches, peeled, halved, and pitted
6 firm ripe plums, halved and pitted
3 large firm ripe pears, peeled, halved, and cored

To the boiling syrup, add the fruit and cook it, uncovered, spooning the syrup over it, for 12 minutes, or until the fruit is just tender.

1 cup seedless grapes, stemmed, rinsed, and drained
2 tablespoons fine-chopped preserved ginger (optional)

With a slotted spoon, remove the fruit to a serving bowl. Add the grapes and ginger, if desired.

Reduce the syrup to one-half of its volume, allow it to cool, and sieve it over the fruit. Cover and chill the compote for at least 3 hours.

Cucumbers in Yogurt with Mint
Fresh Corn Soufflé
Green Peas à la Française, page 33
         or
Braised Cabbage
Bulgur Salad
Plums in Orange Gelatin
Oatmeal Cookies, page 250

FOR 4 PERSONS

Another menu for the amateur gardener. All vegetables needed for a given menu cannot be mature at the same time; but sometimes two or three will coincide, and it is then that the backyard farmer preens with pleasure. The bulgur salad, which I serve as a side dish, improves if made a day in advance and allowed to "work." The dessert, of course, is made in the morning. And there you are—several ingredients from your own garden, everything readied ahead of time, and no top-of-stove cooking on a warm summer's evening!

Cucumbers in Yogurt with Mint

DOUBLES / REFRIGERATES

PREPARATION: 30 MINUTES

> 1 cup plain yogurt
> 2 teaspoons fine-chopped fresh mint
> Juice of ½ lemon

Blend the yogurt, mint, and lemon juice. Allow the sauce to "work" for several hours in the refrigerator.

> 4 small cucumbers, peeled, seeded, and halved lengthwise
> Vinaigrette Sauce, page 254

Allow the cucumbers to marinate in the dressing, turning them once, for 30 minutes.

At the time of serving, wipe the cucumber halves with absorbent paper, divide the yogurt among 4 plates and on it float the cucumber, cut side down.

Fresh Corn Soufflé

PREPARATION: 25 MINUTES

COOKING: 30 MINUTES IN A 350° F. OVEN

All ingredients for the soufflé, and its dish, may be readied ahead of time.

Have the side dishes ready when the soufflé is done—a feat easily accomplished if you use timers. I do—as many as I feel I need, so that my kitchen recalls a carillon about fifteen minutes before serving a main-dish soufflé. (I even time serving the soup—about eight minutes before I expect to offer the soufflé.) The reassuring sound of the bells obviates hurry and panic.

> 1¾ to 2 cups fresh corn, cut from the cob, or one 10-ounce
>   package frozen corn kernels, fully thawed to room
>   temperature
> 1 cup milk

In the container of an electric blender, combine the corn and milk and, on medium speed, whirl them for 15 seconds, or until the mixture is smooth. Reserve the corn-milk.

4 tablespoons butter	Pinch of cayenne pepper
4 tablespoons flour	Generous grating of nutmeg
1 vegetable bouillon cube, powdered	¾ teaspoon salt

In a saucepan, heat the butter and in it, over gentle heat, cook the flour, stirring, for a few minutes. Stir in the seasonings.

4 eggs, separated and covered with plastic wrap

Ready the eggs, reserving the whites in the bowl in which you will beat them. Butter a 2-quart soufflé dish.

Reserved corn-milk
Reserved egg yolks, at room temperature

To the hot *roux*, add the corn-milk, stirring constantly until the mixture is thickened and smooth. Away from the heat, beat in the egg yolks.

At this point you may stop and continue later.

Reserved egg whites, at room temperature
½ teaspoon cream of tartar

Beat the egg whites, adding the cream of tartar, until they form stiff peaks but are not dry. Fold the egg white into the corn mixture. Pour the batter into the prepared dish and bake the soufflé at 350° for 30 minutes, or until it is well puffed and golden. Serve it at once.

Braised Cabbage

DOUBLES / REFRIGERATES

PREPARATION: 10 MINUTES
COOKING: 40 MINUTES IN A 350° F. OVEN

For a simpler dish, omit the butter.

1 medium head cabbage, the outer leaves removed, and cut into 6 equal portions

In a flat oven-proof serving dish, arrange the cabbage with as much of the cut surface exposed as possible.

1 cup hot water, in which 2 vegetable bouillon cubes are dissolved 1 cup dry white wine	Butter Salt Fresh-ground pepper

Combine the liquids, pour them over the cabbage and add the butter and seasonings, to taste. Cover the vegetable well.

At this point you may stop and continue later.

Bake the cabbage covered, at 350° for 40 minutes, or until it is tender-crisp. Baste the vegetable occasionally with the cooking liquid.

Bulgur Salad

DOUBLES / REFRIGERATES

PREPARATION: 20 MINUTES
CHILLING TIME: 3 HOURS

1½ cups bulgur (cracked wheat)
3 cups boiling salted water

In a mixing bowl, arrange the bulgur and over it pour the boiling water. Cover the bowl and allow it to stand until cool.

8 scallions, trimmed and chopped fine, with as much green as possible 2 large ripe tomatoes, peeled, seeded, chopped, and drained of excess liquid	Grated rind and juice of 1 lemon 1 cup fine-chopped parsley ⅓ cup best quality olive oil Salt Fresh-ground pepper

In a sieve, press out any water not absorbed by the bulgur. Return the bulgur to the mixing bowl. To it, add these ingredients, seasoning the salad with salt and pepper to taste.

Chill the salad, covered, for at least 3 hours.

Plums in Orange Gelatin

PREPARATION TIME: 25 MINUTES

CHILLING TIME: 6 HOURS

The preparation time does not include preparing the Custard Sauce.

2½ cups fresh orange juice, sieved
2 envelopes unflavored gelatin
¾ cup sugar
⅓ cup fresh lemon juice, sieved

Into the top of a double boiler, pour the orange juice and sprinkle the gelatin over it. Allow it to stand for a few minutes to soften. Heat the orange juice over boiling water, stirring to dissolve the gelatin. Add the sugar and lemon juice, stirring until the sugar is dissolved. Chill the mixture until it is the consistency of egg white.

2½ cups sliced fresh ripe plums, seeded

In a mold rinsed with cold water, arrange the plum slices in an attractive pattern. Pour the thickened gelatin over them.

Custard Sauce (optional), page 258

Chill the dessert for at least 6 hours, or until it is set. At the time of serving, unmold it onto a serving plate; offer the sauce separately, if desired.

Eggplant Caviar with Syrian Flat Bread
Sweet Peppers with Carrot Filling
Green Bean Salad, page 48
Danish Apple Cake

FOR 4 PERSONS

The home-grower may glean the body of this meal from his garden. Syrian flat bread is available at specialty food shops and, I notice, appears increasingly in grocery stores. Split it with a fork as you would an English muffin, butter and brown it briefly under the broiler. Eggplant caviar may also be served with sesame seed wafers. Green peppers with carrot filling come to us from Russia, an attractively colorful dish. Green bean salad is especially tempting made with new beans, best enjoyed when very young.

Eggplant Caviar

DOUBLES / REFRIGERATES

PREPARATION: 50 MINUTES
CHILLING TIME: 2 HOURS

    1 large eggplant

With a fork, pierce the eggplant in several places. Put it on a baking sheet and bake it at 400° F. for 40 minutes. Peel it and chop the pulp.

2 medium onions, chopped fine	¼ cup fine-chopped parsley
4 cloves garlic, peeled and pressed	⅓ cup olive oil Salt
4 medium, ripe tomatoes, peeled, seeded, chopped, and drained	Fresh-ground pepper

In a mixing bowl, combine and blend thoroughly the eggplant, onion, garlic, tomatoes, parsley, and olive oil. Season the mixture to taste. Chill it for at least 2 hours.

Serve the eggplant caviar on individual small plates accompanied by knives to spread it on the Syrian flat bread.

Sweet Peppers with Carrot Filling

DOUBLES / REFRIGERATES

PREPARATION: 25 MINUTES
COOKING: 40 MINUTES IN A 350° F. OVEN

The preparation time does not include readying the tomato sauce.

    4 large firm green peppers

In boiling water to cover, parboil the peppers for 10 minutes. Remove their stem ends, seeds, and internal ribs.

2½ cups grated carrot	Salt
1 medium onion, grated	Fresh-ground pepper
4 tablespoons soft butter	Grated Parmesan cheese
¼ cup bread crumbs	

In a mixing bowl, combine and blend the carrot, onion, butter, and bread crumbs, and season to taste. Stuff the peppers with this mixture and sprinkle the tops with the cheese.

Stand the peppers in a buttered oven-proof serving dish.

At this point you may stop and continue later.

Tomato Sauce (optional), page 253

Bake the peppers, uncovered, at 350° for 40 minutes, or until they are tender. If desired, offer the tomato sauce separately.

Danish Apple Cake

REFRIGERATES

PREPARATION: 30 MINUTES
COOKING: 15 MINUTES IN A 350° F. OVEN

2 pounds apples, peeled, cored, and quartered	1 teaspoon vanilla
	½ cup sugar
Water	Few grains of salt

In a saucepan, combine the apples with sufficient water to start their cooking. Simmer them, stirring gently, for 12 minutes, or until they are tender. Add the seasonings, stirring until the sugar is dissolved.

6 tablespoons butter
3 cups bread crumbs
½ cup sugar

In a skillet, heat the butter and into it stir the bread crumbs and sugar. Brown the mixture slightly, stirring it constantly.

In a lightly buttered baking dish, arrange alternate layers of the crumbs and the apples; finish with a layer of crumbs.

At this point you may stop and continue later.

Whipped cream *or* Custard Sauce, page 258

Bake the apple cake, uncovered, at 350° for 15 minutes. Serve it hot or
at room temperature, accompanied by whipped cream or custard sauce.

Tomato and Cucumber Salad with Feta Cheese
Spinach Pie
Escalloped Eggplant
Nut Cake

F O R 6 P E R S O N S

This Greek menu evokes memories of a summer spent cruising among
the Greek islands of the Aegean aboard a fifty-five foot ketch. Our lunch
consisted, almost invariably, of the salad which begins this meal, bread,
and resinated wine (an acquired taste, but, if lightly resinated, a pleasant drink). I never attempted making spinach pie (*spanakopita*) in our
very simple galley, but the evening meal would sometimes include escalloped eggplant. In the Mediterranean region, eggplant is very small compared with the large variety we know; if you find small ones, use them,
for they are very tender and cook rapidly. The nut cake (*karydopita*)
serves many more than six people, but it freezes for future use.

Tomato and Cucumber Salad with Feta Cheese

REFRIGERATES

PREPARATION: 15 MINUTES

*If you refrigerate the salad, cover it with plastic wrap. Made with one
hard-boiled egg per serving, Greek salad becomes a main dish—as it did
when I prepared it on board the "Rowena."*

Salad greens of your choice,
   rinsed and dried
Ripe tomatoes, cut in
   wedges
Cucumber, peeled and
   sliced
Radishes, trimmed and
   washed
Scallions, trimmed and
   washed

Ripe oil-cured olives
   (or, if preferred, regular
   ripe olives)
Salt
Fresh-ground pepper
Fine olive oil
Feta cheese, crumbled
Lemon wedges

It is difficult to give specific quantities, which will depend upon the size of the tomatoes, cucumbers, and radishes. Prepare what you think will be eaten—then add a little more, for Greek salad wins friends easily.

On a large serving platter, arrange a bed of the salad greens. Over it, arrange, according to your taste, tomato wedges, cucumber slices, radishes, scallions, and olives. Salt the salad very lightly and season it to taste with pepper. Over the salad, sprinkle olive oil. Add a generous sprinkling of the cheese and garnish the platter with lemon wedges.

Spinach Pie

PREPARATION: 20 MINUTES

COOKING: 45 MINUTES IN A 350° F. OVEN

If you should want to double the recipe, it is best to make two pies.

Phyllo (or strudel) pastry is available in specialty food shops. What you do not use in this recipe will keep in the refrigerator for several weeks.

   10 sheets *phyllo* pastry (12 x 15 inches)
   Melted butter

Cut the *phyllo* sheets in half to measure 12 × 7½ inches. Over the bottom of an oven-proof 11 × 7-inch serving dish, spread a sheet of the pastry. Brush it with melted butter. Repeat this step until you have used 10 of the 20 half sheets of pastry.

Two 10-ounce packages fresh spinach, the woody stems removed, washed in cold water, and dried (or two 10-ounce
packages frozen chopped spinach, fully thawed to room
temperature, and pressed dry in a colander)

In a large soup kettle, bring to the boil several quarts of salted water.
Into it, plunge the spinach, allowing it to wilt for 20 seconds. Drain it
thoroughly and chop it coarse. (If you use thawed frozen chopped spinach, the vegetable will cook sufficiently as it bakes.)

4 eggs
1 cup Béchamel Sauce,
   page 254
1 cup fine crumbled feta
   cheese
1 bunch scallions, trimmed
   and chopped fine, with
   as much green as possible

⅓ cup chopped
   parsley
Grating of
   nutmeg
Salt
Fresh-ground
   pepper

In a mixing bowl, beat the eggs lightly, stir in the Béchamel sauce and
feta. Add the spinach and blend the mixture well. In an even layer,
spread it over the *phyllo* sheets. Sprinkle first the scallions and then the
parsley over the spinach. Add a sprinkling of nutmeg, salt, and pepper.

Spread the remaining 10 sheets of *phyllo* pastry over the contents of
the dish, buttering each one as you did in the first step.

At this point you may stop and continue later.

Bake the spinach pie at 350° for 45 minutes, or until the spinach is set
and the pastry is golden. Serve it at once.

Escalloped Eggplant

DOUBLES / REFRIGERATES

PREPARATION: 20 MINUTES
COOKING: 1 HOUR IN A 350° F. OVEN

*Put the eggplant into the oven 15 minutes before the spinach pie. Or,
pre-bake the eggplant for 45 minutes at 350° F. and return it to the
oven, uncovered, for 15 minutes just before serving.*

¼ cup olive oil
2 medium onions, peeled
and chopped
1 clove garlic, peeled and
chopped
1 large or 2 medium egg-
plant, unpeeled and cut
in 1-inch cubes

2 ripe medium tomatoes,
peeled, seeded, and
chopped
½ teaspoon thyme
1 teaspoon sugar
1 teaspoon salt
½ teaspoon pepper

In a flame-proof casserole, heat the oil and in it cook the onion and garlic until translucent. Add the eggplant, stirring to coat it with the oil. Stir in the tomato and seasonings.

At this point you may stop and continue later.

Bake the eggplant, covered, at 350° for 45 minutes; remove the cover and continue baking the dish for 15 minutes. (The eggplant should be moist but not watery.)

Nut Cake

REFRIGERATES / FREEZES

PREPARATION: 20 MINUTES
COOKING: 40 MINUTES IN A 350° F. OVEN

Very rich, very good, and very light.

½ pound soft butter
1 cup sugar
6 eggs
Grated rind of 1 large orange

In a mixing bowl, combine the butter and sugar and beat until the mixture is light. Add the eggs, one at a time, beating each addition. Stir in the orange rind.

1 cup flour
1 cup farina
1 cup fine-chopped nuts
(hazelnuts are used in
Greece)

2½ teaspoons baking powder
1½ teaspoons cinnamon
1 teaspoon ginger
Pinch of salt

In a large bowl mix thoroughly the dry ingredients.

To the dry ingredients, add the liquid mixture, beating the batter until it is smooth. Spoon it into a 9- × 13-inch buttered oven-proof dish and bake it at 350° for 40 minutes, or until a sharp knife inserted at the center comes out clean.

2 cups water	1 lemon, sliced thin
2 cups sugar	Three 2-inch pieces cinnamon stick
	Few grains of salt

Meanwhile, in a saucepan, combine these five ingredients; bring them to a rolling boil over high heat, and cook, uncovered, for 10 minutes. Allow the syrup to cool.

Remove the cake from the oven and at once evenly sieve the cooled syrup over it. Allow the cake to cool before serving it directly from the baking dish, in which any remaining cake may then be stored.

Eggs in Tarragon Aspic, page 25
Casserole of Green Beans
Orange-Glazed Beets
Mixed Green Salad, page 245
Compote of Oranges and Strawberries

FOR 6 PERSONS

The tarragon aspic will please cooks who have an herb garden; but the aspic may also be made with the dried herb. Eggs in aspic provide an elegant and carefree entrée. The bean dish is simple and very tasty —and looks good accompanied by the beets. Thus, from your garden (or from the greengrocer's) you may offer a delicious herb, green beans, beets, and salad.

Casserole of Green Beans

DOUBLES / REFRIGERATES

PREPARATION: 30 MINUTES
COOKING: 15 MINUTES IN A 350° F. OVEN

> 1½ pounds green beans, the stems removed, halved, and
> rinsed in cold water

In a soup kettle, bring to a rolling boil several quarts of salted water.
Into it, plunge the beans; leave them uncovered. After the water has
returned to the boil, cook the beans for 12 minutes, or until they are
just tender-crisp. (The age of the beans will determine their cooking
time.) Refresh them in cold water; drain and reserve them.

> 4 tablespoons butter   Grating of nutmeg
> 4 tablespoons flour   Salt
> 2½ cups milk   Fresh-ground pepper
> 1½ cups grated mild Cheddar
> cheese

In a large saucepan, heat the butter and in it, over gentle heat, cook
the flour for a few minutes, stirring. Gradually add the milk, stirring
constantly until the mixture is thickened and smooth. Away from the
heat, add the cheese, stirring until it is melted. Season the sauce to
taste.

> Reserved beans

Into the sauce, gently fold the beans. Arrange the mixture in a buttered
oven-proof serving dish.

> 1 cup bread crumbs, toasted in 2 tablespoons butter
> (optional)

Prepare the bread crumbs.

At this point you may stop and continue later.

> Paprika

Spread the bread crumbs evenly over the beans. Add a sprinkling of
paprika. Bake the beans at 350° for 15 minutes, or until the dish is
well heated and the crumbs begin to brown.

Orange-Glazed Beets

DOUBLES / REFRIGERATES

PREPARATION: 1 HOUR
COOKING: 5 MINUTES

The preparation time does not require your constant surveillance in the kitchen; beets often require this long to cook. If you prefer, serve the beets without the glaze.

> 9 large beets, scrubbed and cooked in boiling salted water
>   until fork-tender

When the beets are cooked, cool them in cold water, peel, and either slice them or cut them into bite-size pieces. While they are cooking, prepare the sauce.

> 3 tablespoons butter
> ⅓ cup orange marmalade
> 1½ tablespoons vinegar
> Salt

In a skillet, heat the butter and to it add the marmalade and vinegar, stirring to blend the mixture well. Add the beets to the glaze, shaking the pan to coat them on all sides. Season them to taste.

At this point you may stop and continue later.

Over high heat, bring the glaze to the boil and, shaking the pan or stirring constantly, bring the beets to serving temperature.

Compote of Oranges and Strawberries

Hull, rinse, drain, and halve lengthwise 1 pint of strawberries. Arrange the berries in a serving bowl. Halve 3 juice oranges, and holding the halves over the strawberries (so that no juice is wasted), scoop out their pulp. Gently toss together the strawberries, orange bits, and the juice. Chill the dessert for at least 2 hours.

Watercress Soup
Casserole of Green Tomatoes
Green Peas with Mint, page 17
Cornbread, page 236
Fresh Fruit of Your Choice

FOR 6 PERSONS

A menu for late summer when the home gardener wonders what to do with tomatoes not yet ripe. If you also have a stream from which to gather the watercress, the greater part of this meal may be homegrown. I am fortunate in this respect and must admit to the first deadly sin as I take pride in offering three dishes from my own garden. They can be made as effectively, however, with produce from more readily available sources.

Watercress Soup

DOUBLES / REFRIGERATES / FREEZES

PREPARATION: 45 MINUTES

The soup may be served hot or cold.

2 bunches watercress, rinsed and chopped coarse	1 medium potato, peeled and diced
1 large head Boston lettuce, rinsed and chopped coarse	6 cups water
	5 vegetable bouillon cubes
1 medium onion, peeled and quartered	

In a large saucepan, combine these five ingredients. Bring the liquid to the boil, reduce the heat, and simmer the vegetables, covered, for 30 minutes, or until the potato is very tender.

In the container of an electric blender, whirl the mixture on medium speed, two cups at a time, until it is reduced to a smooth purée. Transfer to a second saucepan.

1 cup heavy cream, scalded
Salt
Fresh-ground white pepper

To the purée, add the cream, stirring to blend the soup well. Season the soup with salt and pepper to taste.

Casserole of Green Tomatoes

DOUBLES / REFRIGERATES

PREPARATION: 25 MINUTES
COOKING: 20 MINUTES IN A 350° F. OVEN

A dish prepared quite similarly to Tomatoes in Cream, page 124, but with its own distinctive flavor.

4 tablespoons butter	**Sugar**
8 large green tomatoes, cut	**Salt**
in ½-inch slices	**3 large onions, peeled and**
Curry powder	**sliced**
Paprika	**¼ cup chopped parsley**

In a large skillet, heat the butter and in it, over moderately high heat, cook the tomato slices for 10 minutes, turning them once, until they are limp. More butter may be added as necessary. Transfer the tomatoes to an oven-proof serving dish and sprinkle them with each of the seasonings. Make a layer of the onion, and season as you did the tomato slices. Sprinkle with the parsley.

2 cups sour cream, thinned with ⅓ cup milk

Spread the sour cream evenly over the contents of the baking dish.

At this point you may stop and continue later.

¼ cup bread crumbs
¼ cup grated Parmesan cheese

In a mixing bowl, blend the bread crumbs and cheese. Sprinkle the mixture over the sour cream. Bake the tomatoes at 350° for 20 minutes, or until the sour cream is slightly bubbly.

Mushroom Caps with Purée of Green Peas
Broiled Eggplant Slices
Braised Red Cabbage
Carrots Vichy, page 47
Compote of Italian Plums
Oatmeal Cookies (optional), page 250

FOR 6 PERSONS

A menu from your garden. Like a musical theme with variations, this menu is capable of various twists and changes. Indeed, I feel its most pleasant feature to be the variability of each separate dish, depending upon the whim or inspiration of the cook; a few possibilities are indicated in the individual recipes.

Mushroom Caps with Purée of Green Peas

DOUBLES / REFRIGERATES PRIOR TO COOKING

PREPARATION: 30 MINUTES
COOKING: 20 MINUTES IN A 350° F. OVEN

For the sake of convenience, use frozen peas. If desired, the mushroom stem may be omitted from the filling; in this case, use two 10-ounce boxes of peas and the sautéed onion. One 10½-ounce can condensed

green pea soup may also be substituted for the peas—a big timesaver!
(To facilitate broiling the eggplant, which follows, cook the mushrooms
in the oven at 350° F. and, when you serve them, turn the oven con-
trols to "broil.")

One 10-ounce package frozen green peas, cooked until very
   tender according to the directions on the package
12 large or 18 medium mushrooms

While the peas are cooking, remove the stems from the mushrooms,
cut off their bottoms, chop them fine, and reserve them. Clean the
mushroom caps, if necessary, by rubbing them with a damp cloth.

¼ pound butter, melted

Quickly dip the mushroom caps in the butter. More butter may be
used, if necessary. Arrange them, open side up, in a baking dish.

1 medium onion, chopped fine
Reserved chopped mushroom stems

In any remaining butter, sauté the onion and chopped mushroom
stems.

Cooked peas, drained
Salt
Fresh-ground pepper

In the container of an electric blender, combine the peas and the
onion mixture. On medium speed, whirl the ingredients until smooth.
Season the purée, to taste.

Grated Parmesan cheese

Fill the cavities of the mushroom caps with the purée. Sprinkle the
cheese over them.

At this point, you may stop and continue later; also at this point, the
dish may be refrigerated, covered, for cooking the following day.

Bake the mushroom caps, uncovered, at 350° for 20 minutes, or until
they are tender. Serve them hot.

Broiled Eggplant Slices

DOUBLES

PREPARATION: 10 MINUTES
COOKING: 6 MINUTES IN A PREHEATED BROILER

*If you prefer an Italian flavor, brush the eggplant slices rather heavily
with olive oil into which 1 or 2 cloves of garlic have been pressed. Add
a sprinkling of oregano, in addition to the salt and pepper. The eggplant may be prepared about 1 hour before it is cooked.*

> 2 large eggplants, sliced ½ inch thick
> Soft butter
> Salt
> Fresh-ground pepper

Spread the eggplant slices with butter and season them with salt and
pepper to taste. Arrange them, buttered side up, on a large cookie
sheet.

Broil the eggplant for 6 minutes, or until it is tender.

Braised Red Cabbage

DOUBLES

PREPARATION: 20 MINUTES
COOKING: 60 MINUTES

The cabbage may also be simmered in orange juice.

> 4 tablespoons butter
> 2 tablespoons sugar
> 1 medium onion, chopped
> 1 medium red cabbage, shredded fine

In a deep skillet or flame-proof casserole, heat the butter and to it add
the sugar and onion. Cook the mixture briefly and then add the cabbage, stirring to blend the ingredients well.

At this point you may stop and continue later.

4 allspice berries
3 cloves
Red wine

Add the seasonings and wine, just to cover. Bring the liquid to the boil, reduce the heat and simmer the cabbage, covered, for 40 minutes. More wine may be added as needed.

½ cup golden raisins
2 medium apples, peeled, cored, and diced

Add the raisins and apples and continue to simmer the cabbage for 20 minutes longer, or until it is tender-crisp.

¼ cup orange juice
2 tablespoons vinegar
1 teaspoon cornstarch

Combine the orange juice and vinegar and stir in the cornstarch. Add the mixture to the cabbage, stirring gently until the sauce is somewhat thickened and smooth.

Compote of Italian Plums

DOUBLES / REFRIGERATES

PREPARATION: 15 MINUTES
COOKING: 20 MINUTES
CHILLING TIME: 2 HOURS

The dessert may also be made with prunes, raisins or pears (Comice, Bosc, or Seckel).

18 to 24 Italian (Blue, Purple) plums, halved and pitted

Having prepared the plums, reserve the pits.

Syrup for Fruit Compotes, page 259

Prepare the syrup. Add the plum pits to it; boil the mixture for 5 minutes. Add the plums and poach them, uncovered, for 20 minutes, or until they are tender but still retain their shape. With a slotted spoon, remove them to a serving dish. Remove the pits by sieving the syrup over the cooked plums. Chill the compote for at least 2 hours.

Avocado and Tomato Soup
Tomatoes in Cream
Cornbread, page 236
Green Bean Salad, page 48
Cheese and Fresh Fruit of Your Choice, page 248

FOR 6 PERSONS

"What can I do with these tomatoes?" The anguished exclamation is mine as I face my garden filled with what appears to be a jungle of the delicious fruit. This menu will help a bit. Happily, however, the soup is very un-tomatoish, and the *pièce de résistance* so subtle that one eats, essentially, two tomato dishes without being conscious of the repeated ingredient.

Avocado and Tomato Soup

DOUBLES / REFRIGERATES / FREEZES

PREPARATION: 25 MINUTES
CHILLING TIME: 3 HOURS

The soup may be served cold, if it is a warm evening, or heated over simmering water in the top of a double boiler, if it is a chill night.

> 2 medium, ripe avocados, peeled, pitted, and chopped coarse
> 3½ cups hot water, in which 3 bouillon cubes have been
>   dissolved
> 1 cup plain yogurt

In the container of an electric blender, combine the avocado, bouillon, and yogurt. On medium speed, whirl the ingredients until they are reduced to a smooth purée.

3 medium, ripe tomatoes,   ¼ cup fine-chopped parsley
  peeled, seeded, and   ¼ cup fresh lemon juice,
  chopped   sieved
4 scallions, chopped fine   1½ teaspoons salt
  (the white part only)   Dash of Tabasco sauce

In a mixing bowl, combine and stir to blend well the avocado mixture and these six ingredients. Chill the soup for at least 3 hours.

Tomatoes in Cream

DOUBLES

PREPARATION: 25 MINUTES
COOKING: 30 MINUTES IN A 350° F. OVEN

6 large ripe tomatoes, peeled   Pepper
  and cut in ½-inch slices   1 cup breadcrumbs, toasted
Sugar   in 2 tablespoons butter
Salt

In a buttered oven-proof serving dish, arrange a layer of one-half the tomatoes. Season them with a sprinkling of sugar, salt, and pepper. Over them, spread one-half of the breadcrumbs.

2 tablespoons butter
1 large Bermuda onion, peeled and cut in ¼-inch slices

In a skillet, heat the butter and in it sauté the onion slices until they are limp. Arrange the onion in a layer over the breadcrumbs.

Several fresh basil leaves, chopped (optional)
2 cups sour cream, slightly thinned with milk

Repeat the layer of tomatoes and seasonings, adding the basil, if desired. Over the tomatoes, spread the sour cream and then the remaining breadcrumbs.

At this point you may stop and continue later.

Toast slices

Bake the tomatoes, covered, at 350° for 15 minutes; remove the cover and continue to bake them for 15 minutes longer. Serve them on toast made from substantial white bread.

Fresh Tomato Soup, page 97
Fresh Corn Soufflé, page 104
Braised Chinese Cabbage
or
Broccoli with Lemon Butter
Mixed Green Salad, *page 245*
Fresh Fruit Compote, page 102

FOR 4 PERSONS

This menu allows vegetable gardeners and, perhaps, fruit growers to share the yield of their labor. It is a pleasant meal to offer on a warm evening because nearly everything may be prepared or readied beforehand. The soup, indeed, may be made in advance and frozen, then served hot or cold. The Chinese cabbage or broccoli may be readied several hours before cooking and refrigerated. The compote improves if made the previous day. The soufflé ingredients may be arranged so that your only final concern is assembling and baking the main dish.

Braised Chinese Cabbage

PREPARATION: 10 MINUTES
COOKING: 20 MINUTES IN A 350° F. OVEN

Chinese cabbage, one of my favorite vegetables, is a part of my kitchen garden. Mild-flavored and fast-cooking, it is, unhappily, also a favorite of several garden pests. But with perseverance one achieves very respectable plants, and the care they require is recompensed in eating them.

2 medium heads Chinese cabbage, the leaves separated, rinsed under cold running water, lightly drained, and chopped coarse

3 tablespoons refined sesame seed oil (available at specialty food shops)
2 tablespoons soy sauce

Toss together the cabbage, oil, and soy sauce. Arrange the vegetable in a shallow oven-proof serving dish. Cover it closely with aluminum wrap.

At this point you may stop and continue later.

Cook the cabbage covered, in a 350° oven for 20 minutes. (Bake the soufflé on the upper shelf and place the vegetable on the lower shelf 10 minutes after the soufflé has been started.)

Broccoli with Lemon Butter

DOUBLES

PREPARATION: 15 MINUTES
COOKING: 10 MINUTES

2½ pounds fresh broccoli

Peel the larger stems and split them crosswise. Rinse the broccoli under cold running water.

Cook the broccoli in one inch of salted water in a flat flame-proof baking pan. Turn after the first five minutes. Drain it at once. It will be tender-crisp.

Lemon Butter, page 252
Salt
Fresh-ground pepper

Dress the broccoli with lemon butter, salt, and pepper.

Menus for Autumn

Pumpkin Soup
Eggplant Soufflé
Baked Acorn Squash with Mushrooms
Tapioca Pudding
Oatmeal Cookies, page 250

FOR 4 PERSONS

Nothing could be easier to make than this soup—equally good served chilled in summer. Eggplant soufflé, so elegant and light, is balanced with substantial acorn squash, treated with a fillip of mushrooms. I omit salad, feeling that the meal does not really require one; but, if you wish, offer a simple lettuce salad with Vinaigrette Sauce, page 254. Tapioca pudding was always an autumnal childhood favorite of mine; hence, I imagine, its presence here—still a favorite and so much tastier than the dessert made with a quick-cooking substitute.

Pumpkin Soup

DOUBLES / REFRIGERATES / FREEZES

PREPARATION: 20 MINUTES

Serve the soup hot in autumn, or chilled in summer as an unusual first course.

    2 tablespoons butter
    1 large onion, peeled and chopped fine

In a large saucepan, heat the butter and in it cook the onion until translucent.

2½ cups pumpkin purée   1 teaspoon curry powder
3 cups water   ½ teaspoon dry mustard
3 vegetable bouillon cubes,
    powdered

To the onion, add these five ingredients.

1 cup cream (light or heavy—the choice is yours), scalded
Salt
Fresh-ground white pepper

Into the pumpkin mixture, stir the cream. Season the soup with salt and pepper to taste. Over gentle heat, bring it to serving temperature.

Eggplant Soufflé

PREPARATION: 1 HOUR
COOKING: 30 MINUTES IN A 350° F. OVEN

All ingredients for the soufflé and its dish may be readied in advance.

1 large eggplant, pierced in several places with the
    tines of a fork

Arrange the eggplant on a baking sheet and bake it at 400° for 40 minutes, or until it is tender. Allow it to cool. Peel it; mash the pulp and reserve it.

4 tablespoons butter   ½ cup milk
4 tablespoons flour   1 small onion, grated
2 vegetable bouillon cubes,   Reserved eggplant pulp
    powdered

In a saucepan, heat the butter and in it, over gentle heat, cook the flour for a few minutes. Season the *roux* with the bouillon powder. Gradually add the milk, stirring constantly until the mixture is thickened and smooth. Stir in the onion and reserved eggplant pulp.

4 egg yolks
Salt
Fresh-ground pepper

Into the eggplant mixture, beat the egg yolks. Season with salt and pepper to taste.

4 egg whites, beaten until stiff but not dry

Into the eggplant mixture, fold the egg whites. Spoon the batter into a lightly buttered 2-quart soufflé dish and bake at 350° for 30 minutes, or until the soufflé is well puffed and golden. Serve it at once.

Baked Acorn Squash with Mushrooms

DOUBLES

PREPARATION: 25 MINUTES
COOKING: 40 MINUTES IN A 400° F. OVEN

2 medium acorn squash, split and seeded	8 teaspoons sweet sherry
	Salt
4 tablespoons butter	Fresh-ground pepper

In the cavity of each squash half, arrange 1 tablespoon butter, 2 teaspoons sherry, and salt and pepper to taste. Cover the halves individually with foil and reserve them.

3 tablespoons butter	Grating of nutmeg
½ pound mushrooms, trimmed and sliced thin	Salt
	Sour cream

In a skillet, heat the butter and in it cook the mushrooms, stirring, for 5 minutes, or until they are limp. Season them with nutmeg and salt to taste. Stir in sufficient sour cream just to bind them.

At this point you may stop and continue later.

Place the squash halves in a pan with ½ inch of hot water. Bake them at 400° for 40 minutes, or until they are tender.

When the squash is nearly cooked, bring the mushrooms to serving temperature. Remove the foil from the prepared squash and fill each cavity with an equal quantity of the mushrooms.

Tapioca Pudding

DOUBLES / REFRIGERATES

PREPARATION: 3¼ HOURS

COOKING: 20 MINUTES IN A 325° F. OVEN

Note that you are not imprisoned in the kitchen for the entire preparation time.

2 cups milk
½ cup pearl tapioca

In the top of a double boiler, combine the milk and tapioca; allow it to stand, refrigerated, overnight. Cook the mixture over simmering water for 3 hours. Allow it to cool.

3 egg yolks, beaten
⅓ cup sugar
Grated rind and juice of ½ lemon

Into the tapioca, stir these four ingredients.

3 egg whites, beaten until stiff but not dry
Lemon-Brandy Sauce, page 259

Fold the egg white into the tapioca mixture. Spoon the pudding into a lightly buttered 2-quart soufflé dish and bake it at 325° for 20 minutes. Serve it cold or at room temperature, with lemon-brandy sauce, if desired.

Broccoli Bisque
Tomato Aspic
Curried Brussels Sprouts
Bulgur Salad, page 106
Baked Pears with Ginger Marmalade

FOR 6 PERSONS

A menu for early autumn, when tomatoes are still available and Brussels sprouts are first appearing, and when the days may yet be warm enough to make a cool meal attractive. This meal serves equally well for summer dining. The Brussels sprouts should be cooked at the time of serving; everything else may be prepared in advance.

Broccoli Bisque

DOUBLES / REFRIGERATES / FREEZES

PREPARATION: 35 MINUTES

   3 tablespoons butter
   1 rib celery, chopped
   6 scallions, trimmed and chopped, with as much
      green as possible

In a large saucepan, heat the butter and in it, over medium heat, cook the celery and scallions, covered, for 5 minutes, or until they are wilted.

   1 bunch broccoli, chopped; or two 10-ounce packages
      frozen chopped broccoli
   2 cups water
   3 vegetable bouillon cubes

To the contents of the saucepan, add the broccoli, water, and bouillon cubes. Bring the vegetables to the boil and cook, covered, for 20 minutes, or until the broccoli is very tender.

In the container of an electric blender, on medium speed, whirl the mixture for 15 seconds, or until the purée is smooth. Return it to a large saucepan.

1½ cups light cream, scalded
Salt
Fresh-ground white pepper

Stir in the cream and season the bisque to taste.

The soup may be served hot or cold; for this menu, I suggest its being served hot. Reheat it in the top of a double boiler over simmering water.

Tomato Aspic

DOUBLES / REFRIGERATES

PREPARATION: 1 HOUR
CHILLING TIME: 6 HOURS

4 tablespoons butter
3 ribs celery, chopped, with some of their leaves
1 clove garlic, peeled and chopped
2 medium onions, peeled and chopped

In a large saucepan or soup kettle, heat the butter and in it cook the celery, garlic, and onion, covered, for 10 minutes, or until they are tender.

5 medium tomatoes, chopped coarse	1 bay leaf, crumbled
	2 cloves
3 cups tomato juice	¾ teaspoon tarragon
1 tablespoon tomato paste	1 teaspoon sugar
Grated rind and juice of 1 lemon	1 teaspoon salt
1 tablespoon Worcestershire sauce	½ teaspoon pepper

To the contents of the saucepan, add these twelve ingredients and simmer the mixture, covered, for 40 minutes.

2 envelopes plus 1 teaspoon unflavored gelatin
1 cup tomato juice

In a large mixing bowl, sprinkle the gelatin over the tomato juice and allow it to soften. Into the gelatin, sieve the hot tomato mixture, discarding the residue and stirring to dissolve the gelatin. Adjust the seasoning. Allow the aspic to cool.

3 ribs celery, diced

Meanwhile, drop the celery into boiling salted water for 15 seconds; refresh it in cold water and drain well. Stir it into the aspic.

Salad greens (optional)

Pour the aspic into a lightly oiled 2-quart mold or serving bowl. Chill it for 6 hours, or until it is set. To serve, unmold it, if desired, onto a bed of salad greens.

Curried Brussels Sprouts

DOUBLES

PREPARATION: 25 MINUTES
COOKING: 15 MINUTES

The sauce may be made ahead of time. For those desiring a plainer vegetable, cook the Brussels sprouts as suggested, adding to the cooking water 1 bay leaf and 2 vegetable bouillon cubes; drain the sprouts and serve them accompanied by a well-operating pepper mill.

4 tablespoons butter	2 cups hot milk, in which 2
1 medium onion, peeled	vegetable bouillon cubes
and chopped	are dissolved
1½ teaspoons curry	Grating of nutmeg
powder	Salt
3 tablespoons flour	Fresh-ground pepper

In the top of a double boiler, heat the butter and in it cook the onion until it is translucent. Stir in the curry powder and flour and, over gentle heat, cook the mixture for a few minutes. Gradually add the milk, stirring constantly until the mixture is thickened and smooth. Stir in the seasonings to taste. You may reheat the sauce over hot water at the time of serving.

2 quarts Brussels sprouts, trimmed and rinsed in cold water

Prepare the Brussels sprouts.

At this point you may stop and continue later.

In boiling salted water to cover, cook the sprouts, uncovered, for 15 minutes, or until they are tender-crisp. Refresh them quickly in cold water. Arrange them in a warmed serving plate and pour the sauce over them.

Baked Pears with Ginger Marmalade

DOUBLES / REFRIGERATES

PREPARATION: 35 MINUTES
COOKING: 20 MINUTES IN A 375° F. OVEN

2 cups water	½ lemon, sliced thin
1 cup sugar	Pinch of salt
1 piece fresh ginger root the size of a walnut, grated	

In a saucepan, combine these five ingredients and, over high heat, bring them to a rolling boil for 5 minutes, uncovered. Remove the syrup from the heat.

6 large firm, ripe pears, peeled, halved lengthwise, and cored
Ginger marmalade
Whipped cream (optional)

In an oven-proof serving dish, arrange the pears, cavity side up. Over them, sieve the syrup. Bake the pears, uncovered, at 375° for 20 minutes, or until they are just tender. Fill the cavities with a little ginger marmalade and allow them to cool before chilling them. Serve them, if desired, accompanied by a bowl of whipped cream.

Cabbage Soup
Corn Pudding
Cauliflower
Cream Biscuits, page 237
Assorted Cheese and Fresh Fruit of Your Choice,
    page 248

FOR 6 PERSONS

Autumn vegetables, a hot bread, and a simple dessert—I suggest apples and pears with a good, sharp Cheddar—compose this homely meal, cozy, satisfying, and without pretension. Like several other dishes in this book, corn pudding recalls my childhood when Mother, always the best cook we ever had, made it according to this recipe.

Cabbage Soup

DOUBLES / REFRIGERATES / FREEZES

PREPARATION: 40 MINUTES

    4 tablespoons butter
    1 large onion, peeled and chopped
    1 medium carrot, scraped and grated
    1 medium parsnip, scraped and grated

In a large saucepan, heat the butter and in it cook the three vegetables until the onion is translucent.

    1 small cabbage (about   4 vegetable bouillon cubes,
        ¾ pound), shredded   powdered
        fine   1 bay leaf
    4 cups water   1 teaspoon powdered cumin

To the contents of the saucepan, add these five ingredients. Bring the liquid to the boil, reduce the heat, and simmer the mixture, covered, for 20 minutes.

Salt
Fresh-ground pepper
Sour cream (optional)

Remove the bay leaf. Season the soup with salt and pepper to taste. Serve it hot, garnished, if desired, with a dollop of sour cream.

Corn Pudding

PREPARATION: 20 MINUTES

COOKING: 45 MINUTES IN A 325° F. OVEN

A fine way to use leftover cooked corn.

2 cups fresh or cooked corn, cut from the ear	2 cups milk, scalded and slightly cooked
2 eggs	1 teaspoon sugar
1 tablespoon butter, melted	1 teaspoon salt
	¼ teaspoon white pepper

In a mixing bowl, combine all of the ingredients and blend the mixture thoroughly, with a rotary beater.

Pour the mixture into a buttered oven-proof serving dish.

At this point you may stop and continue later.

Place the dish in a pan containing ½-inch of hot water. Bake the corn pudding at 325° for 45 minutes, or until it is somewhat risen and set. Serve it at once.

Cauliflower

PREPARATION: 5 MINUTES
COOKING: 20 MINUTES

The preparation time does not include making any of the suggested sauces.

1 large head cauliflower, trimmed of its leaves and stalk; rinsed

Prepare the cauliflower. In a saucepan large enough to cook the cauli-flower whole, measure 1-inch of lightly salted water.

At this point you may stop and continue later.

Lemon Butter, page 252 *or*	Salt
Hollandaise Sauce, page 252 *or*	Fresh-ground white pepper
Mornay Sauce, page 256	

Bring the water to the boil. Into it, lower the cauliflower. Cook the vegetable, covered, for 15 minutes, or until it is tender-crisp. Drain it well, arrange it on a serving plate, garnish with the dressing of your choice (my preference, for this menu, is lemon butter), and season lightly with salt and pepper.

Mushroom Caps with Purée of Green Peas, page 119
Baked Stuffed Eggplant, Italian Style
Green Bean Salad, page 48
Ann Kratochvil's Cheesecake

FOR 6 PERSONS

Ann's is one of the best—and easiest—cheesecakes I know. It presents beautifully and provides a festive ending to this rather elegant menu.

Baked Stuffed Eggplant, Italian Style

DOUBLES / REFRIGERATES (SEE BELOW)

PREPARATION: 40 MINUTES
COOKING: 30 MINUTES IN A 350° F. OVEN

> 3 small eggplant, halved lengthwise, the pulp removed to
> yield a ½-inch shell; reserve the shells

Chop the eggplant pulp fine.

⅓ cup olive oil
1 medium onion, peeled and chopped
2 cloves garlic, peeled and chopped

In a large skillet, heat the olive oil and in it cook the eggplant pulp, onion, and garlic, stirring, for 5 minutes.

1½ cups breadcrumbs
¼ cup olive oil
12 pitted ripe olives, chopped
½ cup grated Fontina cheese (or Swiss cheese)
⅓ cup fine-chopped parsley

Juice of 1 lemon
½ teaspoon basil
¼ teaspoon Italian-style red pepper flakes
2 vegetable bouillon cubes, powdered

To the eggplant pulp, add these nine ingredients, stirring to blend well. Fill the reserved eggplant shells with this mixture.

6 to 12 slices tomato, peeled
Salt
Fresh-ground pepper
Grated Parmesan cheese

Arrange one or two slices of tomato on each eggplant shell. Add a light sprinkling of salt, pepper, and grated cheese. Arrange the eggplant shells on a lightly oiled baking sheet and cover them with plastic wrap.

At this point you may stop and continue later. (Also, at this point the eggplant shells may be refrigerated overnight.)

Bake the eggplant shells at 350° for 30 minutes.

Ann Kratochvil's Cheesecake

DOUBLES / REFRIGERATES / FREEZES

PREPARATION: 20 MINUTES
CHILLING TIME: 6 HOURS

This delicious, very rich dessert is contributed by my next-door country neighbor. It doubles very easily and is ideal for buffet entertaining.

Ladyfingers (about 18)
Line a 1½-quart soufflé dish with ladyfingers.

One 8-ounce package cream   2 tablespoons fresh lemon
  cheese, at room   juice, sieved
  temperature   Grated rind of ½ lemon
¼ cup sugar   Few grains salt

In a mixing bowl, using a rotary beater, whip together these five ingredients until light.

1 cup heavy cream, whipped

Fold the whipped cream into the cream cheese mixture.

Spoon the mixture into the soufflé dish and refrigerate it for at least 6 hours. Or you may freeze and keep it as you would ice cream.

When the recipe is doubled, make it in a spring-form pan, so that the completed cake may be removed and served as if it were molded.

Fresh fruit of your choice, cut up (optional)

Serve the cheesecake, if desired, garnished with sliced fresh fruit.

Lentil Soup
Mushrooms in Tomato Sauce
Kohlrabi
Salad, page 245
Pumpkin Custard

FOR 4 PERSONS

Lentil soup is substantial and warming on a brisk fall evening. The main dish, called *champignons lyonnaises* in its native France, is, as you see, a glorification of mushrooms. If kohlrabi is unavailable, substitute young turnips, peeled, boiled for 15 minutes, or until just tender, well buttered, and seasoned with salt and pepper. What could be more autumnal than pumpkin? Pumpkin custard offers a novel way of serving this seasonal vegetable.

Lentil Soup

DOUBLES / REFRIGERATES / FREEZES

PREPARATION: 1½ HOURS

4 tablespoons butter
2 medium onions, peeled
  and chopped
2 ribs celery, cut in large
  dice

2 medium carrots, scraped and
  cut in ⅛-inch slices
2 cloves garlic, peeled and
  chopped fine

In a large saucepan, heat the butter and in it cook these four vegetables, stirring, for 10 minutes.

2 large ripe tomatoes, peeled, seeded, and chopped
½ teaspoon oregano
6 cups water
3 vegetable bouillon cubes

To the sautéed vegetables, add these four ingredients. Bring the liquid to the boil.

2 cups (1 pound) quick-cooking lentils
Salt
Fresh-ground pepper

Add the lentils. Reduce the heat and simmer the mixture for 1 hour, or until the lentils are very tender. Season the soup to taste.

Grated Parmesan cheese

Serve the soup hot, accompanied by grated cheese.

Mushrooms in Tomato Sauce

REFRIGERATES

PREPARATION: 1 HOUR
COOKING (OF EGGS): 10 MINUTES

The mushroom mixture—not the completed dish—refrigerates.

4 tablespoons butter	1 clove garlic, peeled and split
1½ pounds mushrooms, trimmed and quartered	1 bay leaf
	2 whole cloves

In a large skillet, heat the butter. To it, add the mushrooms, garlic, bay leaf, and cloves. Sauté the mushrooms, stirring, for 5 minutes.

2 cups Tomato Sauce, page 253
2 vegetable bouillon cubes, powdered

Add the tomato sauce and bouillon powder. Gently simmer the mushrooms, stirring often, for 20 minutes.

2 tablespoons fine-chopped parsley	1 tablespoon fine-chopped onion
2 tablespoons fine-chopped chives	Salt
	Fresh-ground pepper

Stir in the parsley, chives, and onion. Adjust the seasoning with salt and pepper to taste.

At this point you may stop and continue later.

4 eggs, poached
4 slices buttered toast

While the eggs are poaching, prepare the toast and bring the mushrooms to serving temperature.

On a warmed serving plate, arrange the toast slices. Over each piece, spoon some of the mushrooms. Top the mushrooms with a poached egg. Serve the dish at once. Pass any remaining mushrooms separately.

Kohlrabi

DOUBLES / REFRIGERATES

PREPARATION: 45 MINUTES

Young kohlrabi tops may be rinsed, cooked, chopped, and added to the knobs.

6 or 12 kohlrabi knobs (depending upon their size), the tops removed, peeled, and sliced thick

In boiling, salted to cover, cook the kohlrabi, covered, for 30 minutes, or until it is tender. Drain it.

2 tablespoons soft butter
Salt
Fresh-ground pepper

Toss the vegetable with the butter and salt and pepper to taste.

If desired, the prepared vegetable may be reheated briefly, covered, in a 300° oven.

Pumpkin Custard

DOUBLES / REFRIGERATES

PREPARATION: 10 MINUTES
COOKING: 50 MINUTES IN A 325° F. OVEN
CHILLING TIME: 3 HOURS

1 cup canned pumpkin purée	1 teaspoon grated orange
3 eggs	rind
½ cup sugar	¼ teaspoon allspice
1⅔ cups heavy cream (or	½ teaspoon cumin
one 14-ounce can	Few grains salt
evaporated milk)	

In the container of an electric blender, combine all of the ingredients and, on medium speed, whirl them for 15 seconds, or until the mixture is homogeneous.

Custard Sauce, page 258

Pour the mixture into a lightly oiled ring mold. Set the mold in a pan of hot water, and bake the custard at 325° for 50 minutes, or until it is set. Allow it to cool to room temperature and then chill it before unmolding. Serve the dessert with custard sauce, if desired.

Purée of Rice
Casserole of Mixed Vegetables
Buttered Okra
Muffins, page 235
Dried-fruit Pudding

FOR 6 PERSONS

What childhood memories are evoked by purée of rice! And how pleasant to relive them through this delicate, comfortable soup. A happy contrast is the main dish, so purely vegetable in flavor, and unadorned. If fresh okra is unavailable, frozen will do, but the consistency is not the same; in either case, be careful to *under-* rather than overcook the vegetable. The pudding is as purely fruit-flavored as the casserole is vegetal; make it early, together with the soup, and the principal preparation of the meal is complete.

Purée of Rice

DOUBLES / REFRIGERATES / FREEZES

PREPARATION: 1 HOUR

The soup may be served hot or cold. If desired, a little curry powder may be added to the cooking rice.

2 tablespoons butter
2 medium onions, peeled and chopped
1 medium carrot, scraped and sliced thin

In a saucepan, heat the butter and in it cook the onion and carrot, stirring, until the onion is translucent.

¼ cup raw rice
5 cups water
3 vegetable bouillon cubes
1 bay leaf

To the vegetables, add these four ingredients. Bring the liquid to the boil, reduce the heat, and simmer the rice, covered, for 40 minutes. Remove the bay leaf.

In the container of an electric blender, whirl the mixture on medium speed, 2 cups at a time, for 15 seconds, or until it is smooth.

1 cup light cream, scalded
Salt
Fresh-ground white pepper
Fine-chopped parsley

Add the rice mixture to the scalded cream, stirring to blend the soup well. Season it to taste, and garnish each serving with a sprinkling of parsley.

Casserole of Mixed Vegetables

DOUBLES / REFRIGERATES

PREPARATION: 25 MINUTES

3 tablespoons butter	2 green peppers, seeded and
2 cucumbers, peeled, halved	cut into pieces the same
lengthwise, seeded, and	size as the cucumbers
cut into ½-inch pieces	

In a casserole, heat the butter and in it, over moderate heat, cook the cucumbers and peppers, stirring, for 5 minutes.

3 large ripe tomatoes,	¼ cup fine-chopped fresh basil
peeled, seeded,	(or 1 teaspoon dried basil)
chopped, and drained	1 cup sour cream
6 scallions, trimmed and	Salt
chopped	Fresh-ground pepper

Add the tomatoes and continue to cook the vegetables, uncovered, for 5 minutes. Add the scallions, basil, and sour cream, stirring to blend the mixture well. Season the casserole with salt and pepper to taste.

Toasted, buttered English muffin halves (optional)

Serve the vegetables on the English muffin halves, if desired, or accompanied by homemade muffins.

Buttered Okra

DOUBLES

PREPARATION: 20 MINUTES

   1 pound okra, the stems removed, and rinsed

If the vegetable is (preferably) young and small, leave it whole; if not, cut it in ½-inch pieces.

In boiling, salted water to cover, cook the okra, uncovered, for 10 minutes, or until it is tender-crisp. Drain well and arrange it in a serving dish.

   2 tablespoons soft butter
   1 tablespoon vinegar (optional)
   Salt
   Fresh-ground pepper

To the okra, add the butter, vinegar, if desired, and salt and pepper to taste. Using a rubber spatula, gently fold together the vegetable and seasonings.

If desired, the prepared vegetable may be reheated briefly, covered, in a 300° oven.

Dried-fruit Pudding

DOUBLES / REFRIGERATES

PREPARATION: 45 MINUTES
CHILLING TIME: 6 HOURS

If desired, the pudding may be made with an equal quantity of a single dried fruit: apricots, peaches, pears, prunes.

1¾ cups water	⅓ cup sugar
One 10-ounce box mixed dried fruit	Two 3-inch pieces cinnamon stick
½ cup raisins	Pinch of salt
2 tart apples, peeled, cored, and diced	

In a saucepan, combine these seven ingredients. Bring the liquid to the boil, reduce the heat, and simmer the fruit, covered, for 30 minutes, or until it is very tender.

Remove and discard the cinnamon sticks and any seeds (such as prune pits).

In the container of an electric blender, whirl the mixture, in two portions, on medium speed for 15 seconds, or until it is smooth. Transfer it to a second saucepan.

> Juice of ½ lemon, sieved
> 1½ tablespoons potato flour mixed with 1 tablespoon
>   cold water
> Custard Sauce (optional), page 258

Stir in the lemon juice and potato flour mixture. Bring to the boil, stirring until the mixture is thickened and smooth. Pour the pudding into a mold rinsed in cold water or into a serving bowl; allow it to cool and then chill it for at least 6 hours, or until it is set. Unmold or serve it from the bowl, accompanied by custard sauce, if desired.

Fresh Vegetable Soup, page 57
Peppers Stuffed with Rice and Cheese
Salad, page 245
Apple Tapioca

FOR 6 PERSONS

The delicate flavor of the soup is complemented by the hearty taste of the peppers, which is in turn lightened by the salad (make it one containing several surprises). The dessert is homely, comfortable, reminiscent of childhood—and always a favorite with me.

Peppers Stuffed with Rice and Cheese

DOUBLES

PREPARATION: 30 MINUTES
COOKING: 15 MINUTES IN A 350° F. OVEN

If desired, you may prepare and fill the peppers and then refrigerate them overnight before cooking.

6 green or sweet red peppers, halved lengthwise, and seeded

In boiling salted water to cover, blanch the pepper halves for 5 minutes. Drain them thoroughly. Reserve the liquid.

1½ cups raw natural rice
Reserved pepper liquid plus water to equal 3 cups

In a saucepan, combine the rice and the three cups of pepper water. Bring the liquid to the boil, reduce the heat, and simmer the rice, covered, for 15 minutes, or until it is tender and the liquid is absorbed. Remove from the heat and reserve it.

2 tablespoons butter
1 medium onion, peeled and chopped

In a large saucepan, heat the butter and in it cook the onion until translucent.

¾ cup water	**¼ teaspoon thyme**
2 cups grated Cheddar cheese	**Salt**
Reserved rice	**Fresh-ground pepper**
⅓ cup fine-chopped parsley	**Grated Parmesan cheese**

To the onion, add the water, cheese, reserved rice, parsley, and thyme. Using two forks, gently toss the mixture to blend it well. Season it to taste. Fill the pepper shells with this mixture. Sprinkle them with Parmesan. Arrange the peppers in a baking dish.

At this point you may stop and continue later.

Bake the peppers at 350° for 15 minutes, or until they are well heated and the Parmesan is melted.

Apple Tapioca

PREPARATION: 30 MINUTES
COOKING: 45 MINUTES IN A 350° F. OVEN

2½ cups water
1 cup light brown sugar
¼ cup white sugar
⅓ cup quick-cooking tapioca
3 tablespoons butter

Grated rind and juice of
   1 small lemon
½ teaspoon cinnamon
¾ teaspoon salt

In a saucepan, combine these nine ingredients. Bring the mixture to the boil, stirring constantly.

5 large tart apples, peeled, cored, and sliced thin

In a buttered oven-proof serving dish, arrange the apple slices in an overlapping pattern. Over them, spoon the tapioca mixture.

At this point you may stop and continue later.

Cream

Bake the dessert at 350° for 45 minutes. Serve it warm with cream.

Brussels Sprouts Soup
Pasta with Eggplant Sauce
Mixed Salad, page 247
Apple Mousse

FOR 4 PERSONS

As a devotee of the delights of pasta, I am always attracted by an unusual sauce to accompany it. This one—eggplant sauce—is particularly tasty, I feel. Pasta dishes are enhanced by salads; I suggest a mixed salad with Oil-and-Lemon Dressing, page 256. After such a feast, the airy apple mousse is pleasantly refreshing.

Brussels Sprouts Soup

DOUBLES / REFRIGERATES / FREEZES

PREPARATION: 25 MINUTES

  4 tablespoons butter
  2 pints fresh Brussels sprouts, trimmed and rinsed (or two
      10-ounce packages frozen Brussels sprouts, fully thawed
      to room temperature
  2 medium onions, peeled and chopped

In a large saucepan, heat the butter and in it cook the Brussels sprouts
and onion until the onion is translucent. Stir the mixture frequently.

  2 cups water
  3 vegetable bouillon cubes
  ½ teaspoon powdered cumin

To the Brussels sprouts, add the water, bouillon cubes, and cumin.
Bring the liquid to the boil and cook the sprouts for 10 minutes, or
until they are tender.

   In the container of an electric blender, whirl the mixture briefly
on medium speed, 2 cups at a time (the sprouts should be chopped
fine but not puréed).

  1 cup light cream, scalded
  Salt
  Fresh-ground pepper

Add the Brussels sprouts mixture to the scalded cream. Season the
soup with salt and pepper to taste. Serve it hot.

Pasta with Eggplant Sauce

DOUBLES / REFRIGERATES

PREPARATION: 45 MINUTES

  4 tablespoons olive oil
  2 large onions, peeled and chopped
  2 medium carrots, scraped and sliced very thin

In a large skillet, heat the oil and in it cook the onion and carrot, stirring, until the onion is translucent.

> One 35-ounce can Italian tomatoes
> 1 teaspoon basil
> 1 teaspoon salt
> Fresh-ground pepper

To the vegetables, add the tomatoes and seasonings. Over gentle heat, simmer the mixture, uncovered, for 25 minutes, or until it is smooth and somewhat thickened.

> 3 tablespoons olive oil
> 1 large eggplant, peeled and cut in ½-inch cubes

In a skillet, heat the oil and in it sauté the eggplant cubes, stirring to brown them. (More oil may be added as necessary.)

At this point you may stop and continue later.

Add the eggplant to the tomato mixture and simmer the sauce for 10 minutes.

> 1 pound linguini or spinach noodles (my favorite), cooked
> *al dente* according to package directions
> Grated Parmesan cheese

Drain the pasta well. On heated plates, arrange it in four individual servings. Spoon some of the sauce over it. Offer any remaining sauce separately, together with the cheese.

Apple Mousse

REFRIGERATES

PREPARATION: 25 MINUTES
CHILLING TIME: 6 HOURS

The preparation time does not include readying the lemon-brandy sauce.

> 1 envelope and 1 teaspoon unflavored gelatin
> ½ cup orange juice

Sprinkle the gelatin over the orange juice. Allow it to soften and then dissolve it over hot water. Reserve it.

Grated rind and juice of	¾ cup sugar
1 lemon	1 teaspoon vanilla
4 large apples, peeled and	Pinch of salt
grated fine	

In a mixing bowl, put the lemon rind and juice. Stir the apples into the juice as you grate them (the lemon will prevent their discoloring). Add the sugar and seasonings, stirring to dissolve the sugar. Stir in the gelatin and chill the mixture until it just begins to set.

1 cup heavy cream, whipped Lemon-Brandy Sauce
  (optional), page 259

Into the apple mixture, fold the whipped cream. Spoon the mousse into a serving bowl rinsed with cold water, and chill it for at least 6 hours, or until it is set. If desired, serve the dessert with lemon-brandy sauce.

Avocado and Cucumber Soup
Onions with Cheese in Custard
Cabbage with Celery and Green Pepper
Fresh Pineapple Tart

FOR 6 PERSONS

The soup is elusively delicate (if you wish, add a *little* curry powder to the cooking cucumber). The main dish makes unusual use of a too neglected vegetable—the mild Bermuda onion. The pure vegetal taste, unadorned, is the particular quality of the cabbage dish. A happy

ending to the meal is the tart, contrasting in taste and texture with
what has preceded it.

Avocado and Cucumber Soup

DOUBLES / REFRIGERATES / FREEZES

PREPARATION: 20 MINUTES
CHILLING TIME: 2 HOURS

*Though it is suggested that the soup be served chilled, it is also tasty
when heated (see below).*

2 large cucumbers, trimmed and chopped	1 bay leaf
	6 sprigs parsley
1 small onion, peeled and chopped	2 cups water
	2 vegetable bouillon cubes

In a saucepan, combine these six ingredients. Bring the liquid to the
boil, reduce the heat, and simmer the cucumber, covered, for 10
minutes, or until it is tender.

Remove and discard the bay leaf. In the container of an electric
blender, whirl the mixture on medium speed, two cups at a time, until
it is reduced to a smooth purée. Return the purée to the saucepan.

1 large ripe avocado, peeled, seeded, and chopped coarse
2 cups yogurt
Juice of 1 small lemon
1 teaspoon powdered cumin

In the container of an electric blender, combine these four ingredients.
Whirl them on medium speed for 15 seconds, or until the mixture is
smooth.

Salt
Fresh-ground white pepper

Add the avocado mixture to the cucumber purée, stirring to blend the
soup well. Adjust the seasoning with salt and pepper to taste.

Chill the soup for at least 2 hours, or, if desired, serve it hot, heated
over simmering water in the top of a double boiler.

Onions with Cheese in Custard

DOUBLES

PREPARATION: 25 MINUTES
COOKING: 40 MINUTES IN A 375° F. OVEN

3 or 4 large Bermuda onions, peeled and cut in ½-inch slices

In boiling salted water to cover, blanch the onion slices for 8 minutes. Drain them well. In a buttered oven-proof serving dish, arrange one-half of the onions in an even layer.

¼ cup fine-chopped parsley
6 slices day-old "toasting"" bread, diced
1¼ cups grated Cheddar cheese

Over the onions, sprinkle the parsley and arrange the bread dice. Add a layer of the remaining onion slices. Over the onion, sprinkle the cheese.

1¼ cups milk
3 eggs
1 teaspoon salt
Fresh-ground pepper

In a mixing bowl, combine these four ingredients and blend them well with a rotary beater.

At this point you may stop and continue later.

Over the contents of the serving dish, pour the custard. Bake the onions at 375° for 40 minutes, or until the custard is set.

Cabbage with Celery and Green Peppers

DOUBLES

PREPARATION: 25 MINUTES
COOKING: 10 MINUTES

4 tablespoons butter	3 ripe tomatoes, peeled,
3 cups fine-shredded	seeded, and chopped,
cabbage	with their liquid
1 cup diced celery	2 teaspoons sugar
1 green pepper, seeded and	Salt
chopped	Fresh-ground pepper

In a soup kettle, melt the butter. To it, add the vegetables. Season them and toss to coat as thoroughly as possible.

At this point you may stop and continue later.

Over high heat, bring the vegetables to the steaming point. Reduce the heat and simmer, stirring occasionally, for 10 minutes, or until they are tender-crisp. Adjust the seasoning with salt and pepper to taste.

Fresh Pineapple Tart

PREPARATION: 30 MINUTES

COOKING: 40 MINUTES IN A 425° F. OVEN

The preparation time does not include readying the pastry.

One 9-inch pastry shell, page 237

Prepare the pastry.

**1 medium, ripe pineapple, peeled, cored, diced, and
   thoroughly drained**

Prepare the pineapple.

**1 tablespoon flour
½ cup sugar
½ teaspoon cinnamon
Grated rind of 1 lemon**

In a mixing bowl, sift together the dry ingredients. To them, add the lemon rind and pineapple dice and, using two forks, toss the mixture well.

Crumb Topping for Fruit Tarts, page 245

Arrange the pineapple in the pastry shell. Over it, sprinkle the crumb topping (or you may use a top crust, if you prefer).

Bake the tart at 425° for 40 minutes, or until the topping and crust are golden brown.

Cream of Celeriac Soup
Sweet Potato en Casserole
Mixed Salad, page 247
Pear Tart

FOR 6 PERSONS

In the absence of celeriac, offer Cabbage Soup, page 137. To complement the main dish, offer a mixed salad with many different ingredients: various greens, tomato, green or red onion, and, for crunchiness, water chestnuts. The homely sweet potato does not always receive such glamorous treatment!

Cream of Celeriac Soup

DOUBLES / REFRIGERATES / FREEZES

PREPARATION: 1 HOUR

4 tablespoons butter
3 knobs celeriac, peeled and
   chopped
1 medium potato, peeled
   and chopped

1 medium onion, peeled and
   chopped
1 clove garlic, peeled and
   chopped

In a saucepan, heat the butter and in it cook the vegetables, covered, stirring them often, for 10 minutes.

5 cups water
3 vegetable bouillon cubes

To the vegetables, add the water and bouillon cubes. Bring the liquid to the boil, reduce the heat, and simmer the vegetables, covered, for 30 minutes, or until they are very tender.

In the container of an electric blender, whirl the mixture on medium speed, 2 cups at a time, until it is reduced to a smooth purée. Transfer the purée to another saucepan.

1 cup light cream, scalded
¼ cup fine-chopped parsley
Salt
Fresh-ground white pepper

To the purée, add the cream, the parsley, and salt and pepper to taste. Heat the soup before serving.

Sweet Potato en Casserole

PREPARATION: 25 MINUTES
COOKING: 45 MINUTES IN A 325° F. OVEN

1 cup raw sweet potato dice	½ cup brown sugar
½ cup light cream	½ teaspoon cinnamon
2 eggs	½ teaspoon ginger
4 tablespoons melted butter, slightly cooled	¾ teaspoon salt

In the container of an electric blender, combine these eight ingredients and, on medium speed, whirl them until the mixture is smooth. Pour it into a mixing bowl.

2 cups raw sweet potato dice
¼ cup golden seedless raisins (or more, to taste—optional)

Into the blended mixture, fold the sweet potato dice and raisins, if desired.

At this point you may stop and continue later.

Pour the mixture into a buttered casserole or soufflé dish and bake it at 325° for 45 minutes, or until it is puffed and golden. Serve the casserole at once.

Pear Tart

PREPARATION: 20 MINUTES
COOKING: 40 MINUTES IN A 425° F. OVEN

The preparation time does not include readying the pastry.

One 9-inch pastry shell, page 237

Prepare the pastry.

½ cup sugar	¼ teaspoon coriander
2 tablespoons flour	¼ teaspoon nutmeg
¼ teaspoon cinnamon	Few grains of salt
Pinch of ground clove	

In a mixing bowl, sift together the dry ingredients.

6 firm ripe pears, peeled, cored, and sliced
Grated rind and juice of 1 medium lemon

Gently toss the pears with the dry ingredients, adding the lemon rind and juice. Arrange the mixture in the pastry shell.

Crumb Topping for Fruit Tarts, page 245

Over the top, sprinkle the crumb topping.

Bake the pear tart at 425° for 40 minutes, or until the topping and crust are golden brown.

Baked Mushroom Canapés, page 31
Acorn Squash Florentine
Buttered Turnip
Baked Seckel Pears
Oatmeal Cookies, page 250

FOR 6 PERSONS

A carefree menu; everything preparable ahead of time. There is an elegance, too, in the very simplicity of the meal, one I serve often, knowing that it will be easy, comfortable, and successful.

Acorn Squash Florentine

Any hard squash works well in this recipe.

Follow the recipe for Baked Acorn Squash with Peas, page 165, filling the cavities with three 10-ounce packages frozen chopped spinach, fully thawed to room temperature, pressed dry in a colander, cooked for 5 minutes in 4 tablespoons butter, seasoned with salt and pepper to taste, and mixed with sufficient **Mornay sauce, page 256,** to bind it. Complete the recipe as directed.

Buttered Turnip

DOUBLES / REFRIGERATES

PREPARATION: 30 MINUTES

You may ready the turnip in advance and put it in salted water to cover until you are ready to cook it.

2 pounds white turnips, peeled and cut in ½-inch dice	Salt
	Fresh-ground pepper
	Fine-chopped parsley
Powdered cumin	

Rapidly bring salted water to the boil and cook the turnip for 15 minutes, or until it is tender. Drain and arrange it in a serving dish. Dot the vegetable with butter and season it with a sprinkling of cumin and salt and pepper to taste. Garnish the dish with parsley.

Baked Seckel Pears

DOUBLES / REFRIGERATES

PREPARATION: 15 MINUTES
COOKING: 1½ HOURS IN A 300° F. OVEN

Poaching Syrup for Fruit Compotes, page 259

Prepare the syrup.

12 to 18 seckel pears

Rinse the pears under cold water. Stand them in a casserole, stems up. Pour the syrup over them. Bake the pears, covered at 300° for 1½ hours. Allow them to cool in the syrup. Arrange them, if desired, in a serving dish and sieve the syrup over them.

Mushroom Soup
Spinach Ring
Brown Rice, page 240
Braised Endive with Mornay Sauce
Apple Mousse, page 152

FOR 6 PERSONS

Spinach and brown rice have always been among my favorite foods; their combination here is, I feel, a happy one. Endive with Mornay sauce is so tastily—and easily—elegant. The apple mousse makes the menu pleasingly autumnal. Windfalls from the trees of my small orchard mean that deer will return once more to feed and bed there.

The days are warm and sunny, the evenings clear and crisp—and a
fire burns cozily in the kitchen grate.

Mushroom Soup

DOUBLES / REFRIGERATES / FREEZES

PREPARATION: 25 MINUTES

> 4 tablespoons butter
> 6 scallions, trimmed and chopped fine, with as much green
>   as possible

In a large saucepan, heat the butter and in it, over medium heat, cook
the scallions, covered, for 7 minutes, or until they are soft.

> 1 pound mushrooms, chopped   ½ teaspoon ground cumin
>   fine   1 teaspoon salt
> 3 tablespoons flour   ½ teaspoon pepper

To the scallions, add the mushrooms and cook them, stirring, for 5
minutes. Stir in the flour and seasonings and continue to cook the
mixture for 5 minutes.

> 2½ cups milk, scalded
> 1 cup dry white wine

Gradually add the milk and then the wine, stirring constantly. When
the soup comes to the boil, reduce the heat and simmer it for 5
minutes.

For a smooth soup, whirl the completed recipe, about 2 cups at a
time, in the container of an electric blender. Reheat the soup before
serving it.

Spinach Ring

PREPARATION: 30 MINUTES
COOKING: 40 MINUTES IN A 375° F. OVEN

> 2 tablespoons butter
> 1 medium onion, peeled and chopped

1 large rib celery, chopped
½ green pepper, seeded and chopped

In a saucepan, heat the butter and in it cook the onion, celery, and pepper, covered, for 5 minutes, or until the celery starts to wilt.

1½ pounds spinach, thoroughly rinsed, the woody stems removed, cooked, drained, and chopped; or two 10-ounce packages frozen chopped spinach, fully thawed to room temperature and pressed dry in a colander	Grated rind and juice of 1 small lemon Grating of nutmeg ¾ teaspoon salt ¼ teaspoon pepper

To the wilted vegetables, add the spinach, rind and lemon juice, and the seasonings. Stir the mixture to blend it well.

1⅓ cups bread crumbs
⅔ cup milk
3 eggs, beaten

Into the spinach mixture, stir these three ingredients. Butter a 1-quart ring mold.

At this point you may stop and continue later.

Stir and then spoon the spinach mixture into the prepared mold. Place the mold in a pan of hot water and bake it at 375° for 40 minutes, or until it is set. Unmold it onto a warm serving plate and fill the center with some of the brown rice; serve the remainder of the rice separately.

Braised Endive with Mornay Sauce

DOUBLES

PREPARATION: 25 MINUTES
COOKING: 15 MINUTES

The Mornay sauce may be prepared ahead; the endive should be cooked at the time of serving. The vegetable may also be cooked in an oven-proof serving dish, tightly covered, in the oven with the Spinach Ring;

allow 25 minutes cooking time. If a plainer dish is desired, omit the sauce.

6 to 12 Belgian endives, depending upon their size, trimmed

Prepare Mornay sauce, page 256. Prepare the endive and other ingredients.

At this point you may stop and continue later.

> ½ cup boiling water, in which 1 vegetable bouillon cube is
>   dissolved
> ½ cup dry white wine

In a skillet, arrange the endives. Over them, pour the bouillon and wine. Bring the liquid to the boil and, over medium heat, simmer the vegetable, covered, for 15 minutes, or until it is just tender; turn it after the first 7 minutes of cooking.

> **Prepared Mornay sauce**
> ¼ cup chopped parsley

With a slotted spoon, remove the endives to a serving dish. Over them spoon the sauce and garnish the plate with chopped parsley.

Eggplant Soufflé, page 130
Baked Acorn Squash with Peas
Fresh Corn with Green Onion
Pear Cake

FOR 6 PERSONS

A simple harvest-time meal. Nothing complicated to worry over, everything preparable in advance, yet the menu has, I feel, a special end-of-summer quality which recalls glowing fireplaces and feelings of coziness. Serve the meal with a light, red Burgundy and follow the dessert with espresso made with two or three sticks of cinnamon added to the coffee maker.

Baked Acorn Squash with Peas

DOUBLES / REFRIGERATES

PREPARATION: 45 MINUTES
COOKING: 10 MINUTES IN A 350° F. OVEN

3 medium acorn squash, split lengthwise and seeded
6 tablespoons butter
Salt
Fresh-ground pepper

In the cavity of each squash half, put a tablespoon of butter; season each half to taste. Arrange the squash in a baking dish and bake it at 400° for 40 minutes, or until it is tender.

One 10-ounce package frozen *small* peas, fully thawed to
room temperature
1 cup Mornay Sauce, page 256

Fill the cavities of each squash half with the peas. Prepare the Mornay sauce; cover it well.

At this point you may stop and continue later.

Add the Mornay sauce, in equal amounts, to each squash half. Bake the squash at 350° for 10 minutes, or until it has reached serving temperature.

Fresh Corn with Scallion

DOUBLES / REFRIGERATES

PREPARATION: 15 MINUTES
COOKING: 5 TO 10 MINUTES

6 tablespoons butter
6 ears corn, the kernels cut
from the cob (or two
10-ounce packages frozen
corn kernels, fully thawed
to room temperature)

6 scallions, trimmed and
chopped fine (use only
the crisp part of the
green)
Salt
Fresh-ground pepper

In a skillet, heat the butter. To it, add the corn kernels and scallions. Over medium heat, cook the vegetables, covered, stirring them often, for 8 minutes, or until the corn is tender. Season the dish with salt and pepper to taste.

Pear Cake

REFRIGERATES

PREPARATION: 30 MINUTES
COOKING: 1 HOUR IN A 350° F. OVEN

> 4 firm ripe pears, peeled, cored, and cut in large dice
> ¼ cup orange-flavored liqueur
> ¼ cup sugar

In a mixing bowl, arrange the pear dice. Blend the liqueur and sugar and pour the mixture over the fruit. Allow them to macerate for at least 30 minutes.

> 2 cups flour
> ½ cup sugar
> 4 teaspoons baking powder
> Pinch of salt

In a mixing bowl, sift together the dry ingredients.

> 3 eggs
> ¼ cup milk

In a mixing bowl, beat together the eggs and milk.

At this point you may stop and continue later.

> 4 tablespoons butter, melted and slightly cooled

To the liquid ingredients, add the butter. Combine the dry and liquid ingredients, beating them until the batter is smooth. Stir in the reserved pears and their liquid.

Spoon the batter into a buttered baking dish or loaf pan and bake the cake at 350° for 1 hour, or until a sharp knife inserted at the center comes out clean. Allow it to stand for 5 minutes before turning it out of the dish.

Custard Sauce, page 258 (optional)

Serve the cake warm or at room temperature with custard sauce, if desired.

Cream of Cauliflower Soup
Eggplant Parmesan
Snow Peas with Water Chestnuts
Spinach and Mushroom Salad
Carrot Tart

FOR 6 PERSONS

"What," you will ask, "is Italian eggplant Parmesan doing keeping company with Chinese snow peas and water chestnuts?" I can give no rational explanation, save that we are living, presumably, in a time of international accord and—concerning food of complementary tastes and textures—these dishes go happily hand-in-hand. The whole menu is composed of odd bedfellows; perhaps that is why I like it—it is strange, unexpected, and somehow successful.

Cream of Cauliflower Soup

DOUBLES / REFRIGERATES / FREEZES

PREPARATION: 25 MINUTES

An additional cup of milk may be substituted for the sour cream, if desired.

1 large cauliflower, the leaves removed

In a saucepan, arrange the whole cauliflower. Add ½-inch of water. Over high heat, bring the water to the boil and steam the vegetable, covered, for 15 minutes, or until it is very tender.

3 tablespoons butter   3 cups milk
1 medium onion, peeled and   1 cup sour cream
    chopped fine   3 vegetable bouillon cubes,
3 tablespoons flour   powdered

While the cauliflower is cooking, in a large saucepan, heat the butter and in it cook the onion until translucent. Over the onion, sprinkle the flour and, over medium heat, cook the mixture for a few minutes, stirring. Gradually add the milk and then the sour cream, stirring constantly until the mixture is somewhat thickened and smooth. Stir in the bouillon powder.

Drain the steamed cauliflower, cut it up and, in the container of an electric blender, reduce it to a smooth purée. (A little of the milk mixture may be added to facilitate this operation.)

Grated Parmesan cheese
or
Chopped parsley

To the milk mixture, add the puréed cauliflower, stirring to blend well. Serve the soup hot with a sprinkling of the cheese or parsley. (The soup is also tasty served cold; garnish it with parsley.)

Eggplant Parmesan

REFRIGERATES

PREPARATION: 1 HOUR
COOKING: 20 MINUTES IN A 350° F. OVEN

To double the recipe, it is best to make it twice. It refrigerates for next-day leftovers. Much of this preparation may be done as you wait for the vegetables for the cauliflower soup to cook.

1 very large or 2 medium eggplants (about 2 pounds in all),
    unpeeled and cut in ½-inch slices
Seasoned flour, page 238
Olive oil

Dredge the eggplant slices in the seasoned flour. In a skillet, heat olive oil as needed and in it sauté the eggplant on both sides until it is golden and tender. Drain the slices on absorbent paper.

6 ripe medium tomatoes, peeled, seeded, and chopped (canned Italian tomatoes, drained, will do)	Salt
	Fresh-ground pepper
	½ pound mozzarella cheese, sliced thin
	⅓ cup grated Parmesan cheese
2 cloves garlic, chopped fine	¼ cup olive oil

In a flat oven-proof oiled serving dish, arrange an even layer of one-half of the eggplant; over it, spoon a layer of one-half of the tomatoes, a sprinkling of one-half the garlic, salt and pepper to taste, and one-half of the mozzarella. Repeat. Over the contents of the dish, sprinkle the Parmesan and olive oil.

At this point you may stop and continue later.

Additional Parmesan cheese

Bake the dish at 350° for 20 minutes, or until it is heated through and the mozzarella is melted. Serve it with additional Parmesan offered separately.

Snow Peas with Water Chestnuts

DOUBLES

PREPARATION: 10 MINUTES

In many stores, one can now find fresh snow peas and, sometimes fresh water chestnuts. If you are lucky enough to do so, rinse both of them, shake off the excess water, and proceed with the recipe as directed. A nice, light flavor to accompany the eggplant.

3 tablespoons butter or vegetable oil	Two or three 9-ounce packages frozen snow peas (pea pods) fully thawed to room temperature
One 7-ounce can water chestnuts, drained and sliced thin	Salt
	Fresh-ground white pepper

In a skillet or large saucepan, heat the butter or vegetable oil, and to it add the water chestnuts and snow peas, stirring to coat them well. Over moderate heat, cook them, uncovered, stirring often, for 5 minutes, or until they are heated through. Both vegetables should be tender-crisp. Season them to taste.

Spinach and Mushroom Salad

DOUBLES

PREPARATION: 20 MINUTES

Toss the salad only at the minute of serving; mushrooms drink salad dressing as if it were champagne! A pleasant addition: unflavored croutons (about 1 cup), sautéed in garlic-flavored olive oil.

> **Two 10-ounce packages fresh spinach, the woody stems removed, washed in cold water**

Dry the spinach in a salad drier or with absorbent paper. Cut or tear the leaves into manageable size. Refrigerate them until ready for use.

> **¼ pound mushrooms, sliced thin**
> **Juice of 1 lemon, sieved**

In a container with a tight-fitting lid, combine the mushrooms and lemon juice. Cover the container and gently rotate the mushrooms to coat them with the lemon juice. (Doing so prevents their darkening and gives them added flavor.) Discard any excess lemon juice. Refrigerate the mushrooms.

> **Salad Dressing of your choice, page 256**

Prepare the dressing.

At this point you may stop and continue later.

> **Garlic-flavored croutons (optional)**

In a salad bowl, combine the spinach and mushrooms and toss them with the dressing, adding the croutons if desired.

Carrot Tart

PREPARATION: 10 MINUTES
COOKING: 1 HOUR IN A 350° F. OVEN

The preparation time does not include readying the pastry.

One 9-inch unbaked pastry shell, page 237

Prepare the pastry.

1½ cups grated carrot, packed	½ teaspoon cinnamon
1½ cups milk	½ teaspoon ginger
½ cup sugar	¼ teaspoon nutmeg
2 eggs	½ teaspoon vanilla
1 tablespoon cornstarch	½ teaspoon salt
¼ teaspoon allspice	

In the container of an electric blender, combine the ingredients and, on medium speed, whirl them until the mixture is nearly smooth.

Pour the carrot mixture into the pie shell. Bake the tart at 350° for 1 hour, or until it is set and the pastry is golden brown.

Avocado and Tomato Soup
Baked Cabbage
Carrots in Cream with Mushrooms
Curried Rice, page 241
Fresh Fruit Compote, page 102
Oatmeal Cookies (optional), page 250

FOR 6 PERSONS

This menu centers around the baked cabbage, gathered, perhaps, from your garden in early autumn while it is still freshly tender. The carrots, too, may be of your own planting, and, while they will have grown fat and large, will be fine in the French dish recommended here. The curried rice not only adds substance to a light meal, but also provides a fairly pronounced taste for a menu characterized by delicate flavors.

Avocado and Tomato Soup

DOUBLES / REFRIGERATES / FREEZES

PREPARATION: 20 MINUTES
CHILLING TIME: 3 HOURS

A *richer soup than that on page 123.*

> 3 large ripe avocados, peeled, seeded, and chopped coarse
> 3 cups hot water, in which 3 vegetable bouillon cubes are
>   dissolved
> 1 cup sour cream

In the container of an electric blender, whirl these three ingredients on medium speed until the mixture is smooth. Transfer it to a serving bowl.

> 3 large ripe tomatoes, peeled,   ¼ cup fine-chopped parsley
>   seeded, chopped, and   Juice of 1 large lemon,
>   drained   sieved
> 6 scallions, trimmed and   Tabasco sauce
>   chopped fine (use the   Salt
>   white part only)

To the puréed avocado, add the tomatoes, scallions, parsley, and lemon juice. Season the soup with a few drops of Tabasco sauce and salt to taste.

Chill the soup for at least 3 hours.

Baked Cabbage

PREPARATION: 20 MINUTES
COOKING: 1 HOUR IN A 350° F. OVEN

1 large cabbage, the outer leaves removed, cut into 6 wedges

In boiling salted water to cover, parboil the cabbage wedges for 5 minutes. Drain them thoroughly and arrange them in a buttered oven-proof serving dish.

4 tablespoons butter
1 large onion, peeled and
  chopped
1 cup breadcrumbs

¼ cup fine-chopped parsley
½ teaspoon dried dill weed
  (or 1 teaspoon fresh dill)

In a saucepan, heat the butter and in it cook the onion until it is translucent. Stir in the breadcrumbs, parsley, and dill.

⅔ cup dry white wine
Salt
Fresh-ground pepper

Pour the wine over the cabbage. Season it to taste. Spread the crumb mixture over it.

At this point, you may stop and continue later.

Bake the cabbage, tightly covered, at 350° for 45 minutes; remove the cover and continue to bake it for 15 minutes longer.

Carrots in Cream with Mushrooms

DOUBLES / REFRIGERATES

PREPARATION: 30 MINUTES
COOKING: 15 MINUTES IN A 350° F. OVEN

Carottes à la forestière *is a fine French way of glamorizing this humble root vegetable.*

12 medium carrots, scraped and sliced into ¼-inch rounds

In boiling salted water just to cover, cook the carrots for 15 minutes, or until they are tender-crisp. Drain them, reserving the carrot water, and arrange them in an oven-proof serving dish.

4 tablespoons butter	Grating of nutmeg
½ pound mushrooms, sliced	1 teaspoon sugar
1 tablespoon flour	Salt
1 cup sour cream	Fresh-ground pepper
¼ cup fine-chopped parsley	

In a skillet, heat the butter and in it sauté the mushrooms until they are tender. Stir in the flour. Add the sour cream and, over gentle heat, cook the mixture, stirring constantly, until it is thickened and smooth. Stir in the parsley, nutmeg, sugar, and salt and pepper, to taste. (If the sauce is thicker than you wish, add a little of the reserved carrot water.)

Pour the sauce over the carrots. Cover the dish closely.

At this point you may stop and continue later.

Bake the carrots at 350° for 15 minutes, or until heated through.

Celeriac Rémoulade, *page 68*
or
Baked Mushroom Canapés, *page 31*
Mixed Vegetable Curry with Condiments
Rice, *page 239*
Mixed Green Salad, *page 245*
Cold Pumpkin Soufflé

FOR 6 PERSONS

Celeriac, or celery root, so popular in France, is occasionally available in this country at the greengrocers. It can be grown in your garden— I have done so; harvested in early autumn, it is included here to allow the proud home gardener to offer a little known but delicious vegetable. Before experimenting with the curry, I was dubious of its success; my efforts were rewarded, however, for the dish has contrasts in tastes and textures and the whole is pleasing. The salad, you will find, cools the palate for the delicate, very light soufflé.

Mixed Vegetable Curry with Condiments

DOUBLES / REFRIGERATES

PREPARATION: 35 MINUTES
COOKING: 20 MINUTES IN A 350° F. OVEN

Serve the curry with Rice, page 239, and the condiments listed below.

6 large carrots, scraped and cut into ½-inch rounds	1 bulb fennel, sliced in ½-inch pieces (optional)
8 white turnips, peeled and cut into ½-inch rounds	1 large sweet green pepper, seeded, and chopped
12 pearl onions, peeled	coarse
8 ribs celery, sliced in ½-inch pieces	

In a soup kettle of boiling salted water, cook the carrots and turnips for 5 minutes (after the water returns to the boil); add the onions, celery, and fennel, if desired, and cook the vegetables for 15 minutes (after the water returns to the boil), or until they are tender-crisp. Drain them in a colander and add the pepper.

3 tablespoons butter	2½ cups scalded milk
3 tablespoons flour	Sugar
Curry powder, to taste	Salt
(I suggest 1 tablespoon)	Fresh-ground pepper

In a saucepan, heat the butter and in it, over gentle heat, cook the flour for a few minutes. Stir in the curry powder. Gradually add the milk, stirring constantly until the sauce is thickened and smooth. Adjust the seasoning to taste.

In a large mixing bowl, combine the prepared vegetables with the sauce, stirring the mixture gently to blend it well. Transfer it to an oven-proof serving dish.

At this point you may stop and continue later.

Condiments:	unsalted peanuts, crushed
shredded coconut	golden raisins
cucumber, peeled and	chopped scallions
diced	

Heat the curry, covered, in a 350° oven for 20 minutes, or until it is of the desired temperature. Serve it, accompanied by side dishes of the suggested condiments.

Cold Pumpkin Soufflé

REFRIGERATES

PREPARATION: 30 MINUTES
CHILLING TIME: 6 HOURS

 2 envelopes unflavored gelatin
 ¾ cup cold milk

Sprinkle the gelatin over the surface of the milk and allow it to soften.

One 30-ounce can pumpkin	½ teaspoon cinnamon
purée	¼ teaspoon ground cloves
½ cup sugar	¼ teaspoon nutmeg
Grated rind and juice of	Pinch of salt
1 small lemon	2 egg yolks

In a saucepan, combine these 9 ingredients. Beat the mixture briefly to blend it well. Over gentle heat, cook the pumpkin, stirring frequently, for 10 minutes; do not allow it to boil.

 Add the gelatin, stirring until it is dissolved. Chill the mixture until it begins to thicken.

 2 egg whites, beaten stiff
 1 cup heavy cream, whipped

Into the pumpkin mixture, fold first the egg white and then the cream. Spoon the soufflé into a high-sided serving dish and chill it for at least 6 hours.

(You may make a wax paper collar, about 4 inches wide; oil it lightly, and fasten it with Scotch tape around the top of a regular soufflé dish; remove the collar just before serving the soufflé.)

Hommos with Sesame Seed Wafers
Eggplant Timbale
Broccoli, page 126
Pumpkin Chiffon Pie

FOR 6 PERSONS

A menu which comes from the Middle East (*hommos*), Puerto Rico (eggplant timbale), and the United States (broccoli and pumpkin pie). *Hommos* may not only be prepared well in advance of serving, but also keeps for a long time under refrigeration. The timbale, light and satisfying, is complemented by the broccoli; the meal ends with an elegant and delicate dessert.

Hommos

DOUBLES / REFRIGERATES

PREPARATION: 12 MINUTES

A Middle Eastern appetizer often used as a spread for flat bread, sometimes called pita, *split and toasted lightly.*

One 20-ounce can chickpeas (garbanzos), drained, the liquid reserved
⅓ cup lemon juice
2 cloves garlic, peeled and chopped coarse

In the container of an electric blender, combine these three ingredients and, on medium speed, whirl them, adding a little of the chickpea liquid as necessary, until the mixture is smooth; it should be thick and spreadable.

⅓ cup *tahine* (sesame seed purée, available at specialty food
        stores)
Salt

Add the *tahine* and salt to taste; blend the *hommos* once more.

Serve 2 or 3 tablespoons of the *hommos* on individual plates, accompanied by sesame seed wafers.

Eggplant Timbale

PREPARATION: 30 MINUTES
COOKING: 30 MINUTES IN A 375° F. OVEN

1 very large or 2 medium eggplants

In rapidly boiling water to cover, cook the eggplant whole for 30 minutes. Drain and peel it. In a mixing bowl, mash the pulp until it is smooth.

1½ cups grated Parmesan   ¼ cup fine-chopped parsley
        cheese   Salt
2 eggs   Fresh-ground pepper
6 tablespoons melted but-
        ter, cooled

To the eggplant pulp, add the cheese, eggs, and butter. Stir in the parsley; season the mixture to taste. Using a rotary beater, blend the mixture thoroughly. Spoon it into a 1½-quart lightly buttered oven-proof serving dish.

2 tablespoons butter
1 cup bread crumbs

In a skillet, melt the butter and in it toast the bread crumbs, stirring them frequently. Sprinkle the crumbs in an even layer over the eggplant mixture.

At this point you may stop and continue later.

Bake the timbale at 375° for 30 minutes, or until it is set.

Pumpkin Chiffon Pie

PREPARATION: 30 MINUTES
CHILLING TIME: 6 HOURS

The preparation time does not include readying the pastry.

One 9-inch pastry shell, fully baked and chilled, page 237

Prepare the pastry.

3 eggs yolks, beaten	1 teaspoon cinnamon
⅔ cup sugar	½ teaspoon nutmeg
1½ cups pumpkin purée	½ teaspoon salt
½ cup milk	

In the top of a double boiler, combine these seven ingredients and, over boiling water, cook them, stirring constantly, until the mixture thickens.

1 envelope unflavored gelatin, softened in ¼ cup cold water

Add the gelatin to the pumpkin, stirring to dissolve it. Chill the mixture until it just begins to set.

3 egg whites at room temperature
⅓ cup sugar

Beat the egg whites until they stand in stiff peaks, gradually adding the sugar as you do so.

Fold the egg whites into the pumpkin. Spoon the mixture into the prepared pastry shell and chill it for at least 6 hours or until it is set.

Eggs in Tarragon Aspic, page 25
Cauliflower Pudding
Braised Endive, page 163
Muffins, page 235
Pineapple with Kirschwasser
Oatmeal Cookies (optional), page 250

FOR 6 PERSONS

What pleasure to take from one's garden the cauliflower for this main dish! Indeed, at this season cauliflower is one of our most beautiful vegetables, creamy white framed with delicate green. A seasonal happiness to which I look forward is seeing them sold by roadside vendors on Long Island; they look so tempting that I always buy more than I can use—and then have the pleasure of giving a few to city-bound friends. Endive, like cauliflower, is best enjoyed in autumn.

Cauliflower Pudding

PREPARATION: 15 MINUTES
COOKING: 1¼ HOURS IN A 300° F. OVEN

    2 medium cauliflowers, divided into flowerets

In boiling salted water to cover, parboil the cauliflower for 4 minutes. Drain and chop it coarse; reserve it.

One 13-ounce can evaporated milk	Pinch of mace
	¼ teaspoon summer savory
2 tablespoons melted butter	1½ teaspoons salt
2 eggs	¼ teaspoon white pepper

In a mixing bowl, combine these seven ingredients.

At this point you may stop and continue later.

Reserved cauliflower

Beat the milk-egg mixture until it is frothy. Adjust the seasoning, to taste. Add the cauliflower.

Into a buttered 2-quart soufflé dish, pour the mixture and bake it at 300° for 1¼ hours, or until it is firm and any excess liquid is evaporated.

Pineapple with Kirschwasser

DOUBLES / REFRIGERATES

PREPARATION: 15 MINUTES

1 large ripe pineapple

Remove the leaves and stem end of the pineapple. Cut the fruit into sixths lengthwise. With a sharp paring knife, cut away any remaining tough core. Cut the pulp away from the tough outer skin; allow the edible slice to rest on the skin. Cut the slice into bite-sized pieces, still resting on the outer skin. Arrange the portions on a serving platter.

Kirschwasser, Confectioners sugar

Over the pineapple, sprinkle Kirschwasser. Cover the pineapple with plastic wrap and refrigerate it. At the time of serving, sprinkle the fruit with a little confectioners' sugar. Offer it accompanied by dessert forks.

Menus for Winter

Eggplant Caviar with Sesame Seed Wafers, page 108
Casserole of Parsnips
Butternut Squash
Mixed Green Salad, page 245
Baked Custard with Caramel

FOR 6 PERSONS

If, this past summer, you have had your own garden, now is the time to dig some parsnips, after cold weather has sweetened them. They are especially good in this dish. What childhood memories baked custard evokes—particularly on a reminiscent winter's evening! I recall it as a staple of Sunday night suppers—together with steaming, marshmallow-topped cocoa—happily eaten as my mother read from *Winnie the Pooh* to my twin sister and me.

Casserole of Parsnips

DOUBLES / REFRIGERATES

PREPARATION: 50 MINUTES
COOKING: 30 MINUTES IN A 350° F. OVEN

    1½ pounds parsnips, scraped and cut into ¼-inch rounds

In boiling salted water to cover, cook the parsnip rounds for 40 minutes, or until they are tender. Drain them well and arrange them in a lightly buttered baking dish.

3 tablespoons butter   ¾ cup grated Parmesan
1½ tablespoons flour   cheese
1½ cups milk   ¼ cup fine-chopped parsley

In a saucepan, heat the butter and in it, over gentle heat, cook the
flour, stirring, for a few minutes. Gradually add the milk, stirring constantly until the mixture is thickened and smooth. Away from the
heat, stir in the cheese and parsley.

½ cup bread crumbs

Pour the sauce evenly over the parsnips. Sprinkle the top with bread
crumbs.

At this point you may stop and continue later.

Bake the dish at 350° for 30 minutes, or until the bread crumbs are
browned.

Butternut Squash

PREPARATION: 5 MINUTES
COOKING: 1½ HOURS IN A 375° F. OVEN

  1 very large or 2 small butternut squash, cut into 6 serving
    pieces, the seeds removed

In a baking dish, arrange the squash. Bake it, covered, at 375° for 45
minutes; remove the cover and continue to bake it for 45 minutes
longer, or until it is fork-tender.

Butter
Salt
Fresh-ground pepper

Serve the squash well seasoned with butter, salt, and pepper.

Baked Custard with Caramel

REFRIGERATES

PREPARATION: 40 MINUTES
COOKING: 20 MINUTES IN A 400° F. OVEN

  ½ cup sugar
  2 tablespoons water

In a lightly buttered heavy skillet, over low heat, melt the sugar in the water, stirring constantly. When it has turned golden, pour it equally into 6 oven-proof custard cups.

3 cups milk, scalded
3 eggs, lightly beaten
1 teaspoon vanilla

½ cup sugar
¼ teaspoon salt

Combine these five ingredients and divide the mixture equally among the custard cups. Arrange them in a pan of hot water. Bake the custards at 400° for 20 minutes, or until they are set.

If desired, they may be unmolded before serving.

Dried Bean Soup
Mushrooms Paprika
Brown Rice, page 240
Braised Cabbage, page 105
Cold Prune Soufflé

FOR 6 PERSONS

There is something cheery about a hearty bean soup in winter; it is comforting to both stomach and spirit. Having eaten a "hearty" first course, however, I turn to my preferred practice of light-but-satisfying dining for the remainder of the meal. The first course and dessert are prepared well in advance of serving; the components of the main and side dishes are readied ahead of time for quick and easy last-minute attention.

Dried Bean Soup

DOUBLES / REFRIGERATES

PREPARATION: 3 HOURS

*Do not be disturbed by the lengthy preparation for this Italian classic;
your presence is required in the kitchen for only a short time.*

8 cups water	½ teaspoon marjoram
6 vegetable bouillon cubes	½ teaspoon oregano
2 cups dried white beans of	½ teaspoon thyme
your choice, rinsed	Fresh-ground pepper
½ teaspoon basil	

In a large saucepan or soup kettle, bring the water and bouillon cubes
to the boil and in the liquid cook the beans for 5 minutes. Remove
them from the heat and allow them to stand for 1 hour. Return them
to gentle heat and cook them, adding the seasonings, for 1½ hours,
or until they are tender.

2 cloves garlic
¼ cup chopped parsley
Salt

In the container of an electric blender, on medium speed, whirl one-
half of the beans with some of the bean water, the garlic, and parsley.
Combine the purée with the remaining beans and their liquid. Adjust
the seasoning and bring the soup to serving temperature.

Mushrooms Paprika

DOUBLES / REFRIGERATES

PREPARATION: 30 MINUTES
COOKING: 12 MINUTES

2 pounds mushrooms, quartered
Lemon juice

Gently toss the mushrooms with lemon juice. Discard any excess
liquid. Chill the mushrooms until they are needed.

6 tablespoons butter
1 medium onion, peeled
   and chopped
2½ tablespoons flour
2 teaspoons paprika (pref-
   erably sweet Hungarian
   —use more if you wish)

¾ teaspoon salt
Pinched of cayenne pepper
   (optional)

In a large skillet, heat the butter and in it cook the onion until it is translucent. Into the onion, stir the flour, paprika, salt, and, if desired, the cayenne.

1 cup sour cream
One 8-ounce can tomato sauce
Milk

Add the sour cream and tomato sauce, stirring constantly until the mixture is thickened and smooth. Add a little milk gradually, stirring, until the sauce is of the desired consistency.

At this point you may stop and continue later.

Prepared mushrooms, drained in a colander

To the heated sauce, add the mushrooms and cook them, covered, for 12 minutes, or until they begin to wilt.

Cold Prune Soufflé

REFRIGERATES

PREPARATION: 30 MINUTES
CHILLING TIME: 6 HOURS

*The dessert may also be made with canned purple plums, pitted and
well drained. And, of course, it may be made a day in advance.*

¼ cup prune syrup
1 envelope unflavored gelatin

Sprinkle the gelatin over the syrup and allow it to soften for 10 minutes.
Dissolve it over boiling water.

One 1-pound can or jar stewed   Grated rind and juice
   prunes, well drained, pitted, and   of ½ lemon
   puréed in the container of an   ½ teaspoon vanilla
   electric blender to yield 1 cup   Pinch of salt

In a mixing bowl, combine these five ingredients. To them add the
dissolved gelatin and stir to blend well. Chill the mixture until it just
begins to set.

4 egg whites, at room temperature
½ teaspoon cream of tartar
⅔ cup sugar

In a mixing bowl, beat the egg whites with the cream of tartar. Gradually add the sugar, beating after each addition until the whites stand
in stiff peaks.

   Fold the egg whites into the prune purée. Spoon the mixture into a
lightly oiled soufflé dish or mold and chill it for at least 6 hours, or
until it is set. Unmold the soufflé just before serving.

Baba Ghannouj
Couscous
Cucumbers in Yogurt with Mint
or
Dried-fruit Compote

FOR 6 PERSONS

A menu of pure *fantasie*. It has a Middle Eastern aura, but is not, I believe, authentic. It offers, however, pleasantly contrasting flavors in dissimilar dishes. The couscous you will find delightfully subtle and light. A suggestion for the compote: make it of apricots, peaches, and pears, omitting other fruits; serve it topped with yogurt.

Baba Ghannouj

DOUBLES / REFRIGERATES

PREPARATION: 20 MINUTES
COOKING: 1 HOUR IN A 400° F. OVEN

1 large or 2 small eggplants, pricked with the tines of a fork

On a baking sheet, arrange the eggplant; bake it at 400° for 1 hour. Allow it to cool briefly, peel it, and put the pulp in the container of an electric blender.

5 tablespoons *tahine* (sesame seed purée, avail-
able at specialty food
stores)
Grated rind and juice of 1
small lemon
¼ cup fine-chopped parsley

1 clove garlic, peeled and
pressed
¾ teaspoon prepared horseradish
1 teaspoon salt
½ teaspoon fresh-ground
pepper

To the eggplant pulp, add these six ingredients. On medium speed, whirl the mixture to homogenize it. If desired, the *baba ghannouj* may be made in a mixing bowl; blend the ingredients with a fork.

Sesame seed Melba toast (or salad greens)
New raw turnips, scraped and cut into bite-size pieces (optional)

Serve the appetizer with Melba toast or on salad greens and, if desired, the turnips.

Couscous

DOUBLES / REFRIGERATES

PREPARATION: 50 MINUTES
COOKING: 1 HOUR

The vegetables may be prepared in advance of serving and reheated; the grain is best cooked at the time it is eaten. If desired, one 20-ounce can of chickpeas, drained, may be added to the cooked vegetables.

6 medium carrots, scraped
and cut into 1-inch
rounds
6 medium onions, peeled
and quartered
6 ribs celery, cut into 1-inch
pieces
6 small white turnips,
scraped and quartered

1 very small head cabbage, cut
into chunks
½ cup coarse-chopped parsley
8 cups water
6 vegetable bouillon cubes
Salt
Fresh-ground pepper

In a soup kettle, combine all the ingredients except the salt and pepper. Bring the liquid to the boil, reduce the heat, and simmer the vegetables, covered, for 20 minutes, or until they are barely tender. Adjust the seasoning to taste.

At this point you may stop and continue later.

1 1-lb. package couscous (available at specialty food stores)
Tabasco sauce

Prepare the couscous as directed on the package. Reheat the vegetables.
Offer the grain and the vegetables with their broth in separate serving
dishes. Into heated soup bowls, spoon some of the grain; over it arrange
the vegetables and add a generous amount of broth. Allow each person
to season his own broth with a drop or two of the Tabasco sauce.

Cucumbers in Yogurt with Mint

DOUBLES / REFRIGERATES

PREPARATION: 15 MINUTES
CHILLING TIME: AT LEAST 2 HOURS

If fresh mint is unavailable, substitute 1 teaspoon powdered cumin.

3 or 4 medium cucumbers,
  peeled, quartered lengthwise, the seeds removed,
  and cut in large dice
1 medium red onion, coarse-
  chopped
1 cup plain yogurt
Grated rind and juice of ½
  lemon

3 tablespoons fine-chopped
  fresh mint
2 tablespoons fine-chopped
  parsley
Salt
Fresh-ground white pepper

In a mixing bowl, combine the ingredients and blend them well. Season
the salad, to taste. Chill it for at least 2 hours.

Dried-fruit Compote

DOUBLES / REFRIGERATES

PREPARATION: 15 MINUTES
COOKING: 20 MINUTES

*This recipe serves 6 generously; what is not eaten at dinner will be
welcome for breakfast or lunch. If desired, the compote may be made
with boxed dried mixed fruits.*

Poaching syrup for fruit compotes, page 259

Prepare the syrup.

½ pound each: dried apricots, dried peaches, dried pears,
    dried prunes
1 cup golden raisins
Boiling water

In a large saucepan, arrange the dried fruits. Over them, pour the hot
syrup, together with its seasonings. Add boiling water just to cover.
Allow the mixture to stand, covered, for 6 hours.
    Bring the liquid to the boil and simmer the fruit, uncovered, until
it is just tender. With a slotted spoon, remove it to a serving bowl.
Over high heat, reduce the liquid until it is slightly syrupy; sieve it over
the fruit. Allow the dish to cool before chilling it.

Sour cream (optional)

If desired, garnish each serving with sour cream.

Potato Soup, page 42
Braised Vegetables Provençale
Wheat Germ Muffins, page 236
Mixed Green Salad, page 245
Cheese
Spinach and Orange Tart

FOR 6 PERSONS

With the exception of the muffins, this is a French menu: the potato
soup recipe is one I gleaned in France; the braised vegetables and tart
both derive from Provence; our Gallic cousins are almost as fond of

green salad as we are in this country; and nothing could be more French than cheese (a French cheese, of course) served as a *plat* unto itself (see below for a few suggestions). For the purpose of this menu, bake the muffins before cooking the Braised Vegetables Provençale; keep them well wrapped in foil and reheat them briefly, with the main dish, before serving them. Or, you may prefer a good French bread for this French meal—especially good with the cheese course. You will enjoy a full-bodied red wine with the meal.

Braised Vegetables Provençale

DOUBLES

PREPARATION: 30 MINUTES
COOKING: 1 HOUR IN A 350° F. OVEN

One 10-ounce package frozen cut green beans

2 large carrots, scraped and cut in ¼-inch rounds

1 large eggplant, unpeeled and cut into 1-inch cubes

3 cloves garlic, peeled and chopped fine

2 large onions, peeled and chopped

One 10-ounce package frozen peas

1 green pepper, seeded and chopped

4 ripe medium tomatoes, peeled, seeded and chopped

2 large zucchini, trimmed and cut in ½-inch rounds

2 teaspoons salt

½ teaspoon pepper

⅓ cup olive oil

In a large mixing or salad bowl, combine the ingredients and toss to blend them well. Arrange the vegetables in an oven-proof serving casserole.

At this point you may stop and continue later.

Bake the vegetables, covered, at 350° for 45 minutes; remove the cover and continue to cook them for 15 minutes longer.

Cheese

Serve the cheese of your choice with either French bread or unflavored Melba toast and a little sweet butter. Recommended cheeses for this menu: Brie, Camembert, Bleu de Bresse, Pipo Crème, or Roquefort.

Spinach and Orange Tart

PREPARATION: 25 MINUTES
COOKING: 20 MINUTES IN A 450° F. OVEN

A conversation maker? No, stopper! Delicious. The preparation time does not include readying the pastry.

One 9-inch unbaked pastry shell, page 237

Prepare the pastry shell.

> 1 cup light cream
> 3 egg yolks
> ¼ cup sugar
> Few grains of salt

In the top of a double boiler, using a rotary beater, blend the cream, egg yolks, sugar, and salt.

Over gently boiling water, cook the custard, stirring constantly, until it coats the spoon.

> **Two 10-ounce packages frozen chopped spinach, fully thawed to room temperature and pressed dry in a colander**
> **Grated rind of 1 small lemon**
> **1 teaspoon vanilla**

To the custard, add the spinach, lemon rind, and vanilla, stirring the mixture until it is well blended.

> **1 cup orange marmalade, melted**

Into the pastry shell, spoon an even layer of one-third of the spinach mixture. Over it, spread one-half of the marmalade. Repeat. Finish with a layer of the remaining spinach mixture.

Bake the tart at 450° for 20 minutes, or until the custard is set and the pastry is golden. Allow the tart to cool and serve it at room temperature.

Leeks in Piquant Sauce, page 50
Carrot Souffle
Braised Fennel
Parsleyed Potatoes
Sherry Gelatin
Oatmeal Cookies (optional), page 250

FOR 4 PERSONS

The leeks may be served hot or cold. The soufflé is easy; ingredients, as with all main-dish soufflés in this book, may be readied ahead of time for last-minute assembly. Fennel provides an interesting contrast in flavor, while the potatoes, served piping hot, give substance to the meal. The dessert, one of my favorites, is refreshing and unusual.

Carrot Souffle

PREPARATION: 20 MINUTES
COOKING: 30 MINUTES IN A 350° F. OVEN

All ingredients for the soufflé, and its dish, may be readied ahead of time.

4 tablespoons butter	Generous grating of nutmeg
4 tablespoons flour	1 teaspoon salt
½ cup milk	¼ teaspoon pepper
4 egg yolks	
4 large carrots, scraped and grated fine	

In a saucepan, heat the butter and in it, over gentle heat, cook the flour for a few minutes, stirring. Gradually add the milk, stirring constantly (the mixture will be thick). Away from the heat, stir in first the egg yolks, then the carrot, and finally the seasonings.

4 egg whites, beaten until stiff

Into the egg white, fold a little of the carrot mixture. Then fold all of the egg white into the carrot mixture. Spoon the batter into a lightly buttered soufflé dish and bake it at 350° for 30 minutes, or until it is well puffed and golden. Serve the soufflé at once.

Braised Fennel

PREPARATION: 10 MINUTES
COOKING: 25 MINUTES

3 medium bulbs fennel, trimmed and halved	Butter
2 vegetable bouillon cubes, powdered	1 teaspoon sugar
	¾ cup water

In a skillet, arrange the fennel with the cut side up. Sprinkle it with the bouillon powder. Add a slice of butter to each piece. Season each with a sprinkling of the sugar. Add the water.

At this point you may stop and continue later.

Over high heat, bring the liquid to the boil; reduce the heat and simmer the vegetable, covered, for 20 minutes, or until it is tender-crisp. Turn it once. Remove the cover and, over high heat, reduce the liquid until it is slightly thickened. Arrange the fennel on a warm serving plate and pour the pan juices over it.

Parsleyed Potatoes

DOUBLES / REFRIGERATES

PREPARATION: 5 MINUTES
COOKING: 20 MINUTES

6 medium potatoes

Scrub and, if you prefer, peel the potatoes. If you peel them, put them in cold water to prevent their darkening.

Boiling salted water	Fresh-ground pepper
3 tablespoons soft butter	¼ cup fine-chopped parsley
Salt	

In boiling salted water to cover, cook the potatoes, covered, for 20 minutes, or until they are fork-tender. Drain them. Cut them into eighths. Toss them with the butter, season them to taste, and sprinkle them with the parsley.

Sherry Gelatin

REFRIGERATES

PREPARATION: 15 MINUTES
CHILLING TIME: 6 HOURS

The preparation time does not include readying the sauce.

2 envelopes unflavored gelatin, softened in ¼ cup cold water
1 cup boiling water
¾ cup sugar
Pinch of salt

To the softened gelatin, add the boiling water, sugar, and salt; stir the mixture until the gelatin is dissolved.

> 1½ cups dry sherry
> 1½ cups fresh orange juice, sieved
> 2 tablespoons fresh lemon juice sieved
> Custard Sauce, page 258

Add the sherry and fruit juices. Pour the mixture into a mold rinsed with cold water. Chill the dessert for at least 6 hours, or until it is set. Unmold it and offer it, if desired, with custard sauce.

Artichokes
Broccoli in Cheese Custard
Carrots Vichy, page 47
Green Peas with Scallions
Dried-fruit Compote, page 193
Oatmeal Cookies, page 250

FOR 6 PERSONS

The artichokes may be served hot or at room temperature (they lack full flavor if served cold); if served hot, they are particularly good with Lemon Butter, page 252. The main plate is attractive to the eyes: the dark and light greens of broccoli and peas, the yellow custard, and the orange carrots. The compote should be served slightly chilled, so that it is fresh but not ice-cold.

Artichokes

DOUBLES / REFRIGERATES

PREPARATION: 40 MINUTES

This recipe is the contribution of Jean Westbrook, a close friend of long standing, who "house-sat" for me two summers when I had the opportunity to visit the Aegean islands and to go on safari in equatorial Africa.

6 medium-large artichokes

Select fresh-looking, well-shaped artichokes. Their size will be a matter of availability or your choice. Remove the stems so that they stand straight; with scissors, cut off the prickly tops of the outer leaves; under cold running water, rinse them thoroughly.

2 tablespoons cider vinegar	2 tablespoons sugar
¾ teaspoon oregano	1½ teaspoons salt
¾ teaspoon red pepper flakes	8 peppercorns
	Water
¾ teaspoon thyme	

In a kettle large enough to hold the artichokes standing in a single layer, combine the spices and seasonings. Over them, arrange the artichokes. Add sufficient water to cover them halfway. Over high heat, bring the liquid to the boil; reduce the heat and cook the artichokes, covered, for 25 minutes, or until the outer leaves are easily removed. Drain the artichokes in a colander, standing them upside down.

If the artichokes are to be served hot, offer them at once, accompanied by Lemon Butter, page 252, or Vinaigrette Sauce, page 254.

If the artichokes are to be served cold, refresh them under cold water and chill them until 30 minutes before they are to be used. Offer them with vinaigrette sauce, which, I feel, should always be at room temperature.

Broccoli in Cheese Custard

PREPARATION: 20 MINUTES

COOKING: 30 MINUTES IN A 350° F. OVEN

2 pounds broccoli, the heavy stems peeled and split; well rinsed
(or three 10-ounce packages frozen broccoli spears)

In boiling salted water, cook the broccoli until it is just tender. Drain
it in a colander.

4 eggs, beaten	1 teaspoon Worcestershire
1 cup milk	sauce
1½ cups grated Cheddar	¼ teaspoon white pepper
cheese	

While the broccoli is cooking, prepare the custard. In a mixing bowl,
combine and blend these five ingredients.

In a buttered baking dish, arrange the broccoli in a single layer.

At this point you may stop and continue later.

Place the baking dish in a pan of hot water to the depth of one-half
inch. Add the custard, allowing as much as possible of the broccoli to
show. Bake the dish at 350° for 30 minutes, or until the custard is set.

Green Peas with Scallions

DOUBLES

PREPARATION: 10 MINUTES (ASSUMING YOU USE FROZEN PEAS)

*Little hope, I fear, of finding fresh peas at this season; if you do, buy 3
pounds of them. I prefer very small frozen peas, which barely require
cooking, once thawed. But "regular size" frozen peas are fine, too.*

Two 10-ounce packages frozen peas, cooked according to the directions on the package (do not overcook them); drained in a colander	2 tablespoons soft butter
	1 teaspoon sugar
	Salt
	Fresh-ground pepper
1 bunch scallions, trimmed and sliced, with the crisp green part	

In a mixing bowl or serving dish, combine the hot cooked peas, the scallions, butter, and sugar. Using two forks, gently toss the vegetables to blend them with the butter. Season the dish to taste with salt and pepper.

If desired, the dish may be cooked ahead of time and reheated, covered, for 10 minutes in the oven with the broccoli.

Baba Ghannouj *with Sesame Seed Wafers, page 191*
Mushroom Quiche
Spinach, Italian Style
Pineapple with Kirschwasser, page 181

FOR 6 PERSONS

A menu borrowed from the Middle East, France, and, I suppose, Hawaii, whence most pineapples come to America these days. In fact, pineapples are native to the Caribbean area, where they not only are eaten, but were also symbolic of hospitality, thus giving rise to the pineapple motif in seventeenth century architecture—a conceit taken home by English colonists. The *baba ghannouj* is prepared well in advance; so, too, is the pineapple—indeed, it is improved by steeping in kirsch. The components of the quiche and the spinach, readied ahead of time, allow the cook a carefree meal.

Mushroom Quiche

PREPARATION: 20 MINUTES
COOKING: 30 MINUTES IN A 425°/325° F. OVEN

The preparation time does not include readying the pastry.

One 9-inch pastry shell, page 237

Prepare the pastry.

> 4 tablespoons butter
> 1 pound mushrooms, sliced
> Salt
> Pepper

In a skillet, heat the butter and in it cook the mushrooms, stirring them often, until they are limp. Season them to taste.

> 3 eggs, lightly beaten   ½ teaspoon salt
> 2 cups light cream   ¼ teaspoon pepper
> 3 tablespoons grated Parme-
>   san cheese (optional)

In a mixing bowl, combine these five ingredients and blend them well.

At this point you may stop and continue later.

> Prepared pastry shell

Arrange the mushrooms in an even layer on the bottom of the pastry shell. Over them pour the custard mixture. Bake the quiche at 425° for 10 minutes; reduce the heat to 325° and continue baking it for 20 minutes, or until the custard is set and the crust is golden. Allow the quiche to stand for 5 minutes before cutting it.

Spinach, Italian Style

PREPARATION: 15 MINUTES
COOKING: 5 MINUTES

Garlic, one of man's oldest medicinal herbs, was used by both Greeks and Romans; it remains today one of the best tonics I know. If this dish seems a bit "rich" for your taste, omit the garlic, use less olive oil, and serve the spinach with lemon wedges. The spinach may be prepared for cooking as long as two hours ahead of time.

Three 10-ounce packages
   fresh spinach (or, if
   culled from your garden,
   an equivalent amount),
   the woody stems removed,
   washed in cold water, and
   well drained

¼ cup fine olive oil
3 (or more) large cloves garlic, peeled and chopped
   fine
Salt
Fresh-ground pepper

In a soup kettle, arrange the spinach; over it, pour the olive oil; add the garlic and a generous sprinkling of salt and pepper. Toss the ingredients as if you were preparing a salad.

At this point you may stop and continue later.

Over high heat, bring the spinach to the point of steaming; reduce the heat and simmer, covered, for 5 minutes, or until the spinach is wilted. Drain it, reserving any essence for use in a soup.

Artichokes, page 200
Escalloped Potatoes au Gratin
Braised Lettuce
Indian Pudding

FOR 6 PERSONS

For an interesting cold-day meal, serve the artichokes and vinaigrette sauce hot and the Indian Pudding direct from the oven. A warming and satisfying menu, but one which is light, for the only "heavy" dish is the escalloped potatoes.

Escalloped Potatoes au Gratin

DOUBLES / REFRIGERATES (AS LEFTOVERS)

PREPARATION: 25 MINUTES
COOKING: 45 MINUTES IN A 350° F. OVEN

If desired, 1 medium onion, peeled and chopped finely, may be sprinkled over the first layer of potatoes.

    1 clove garlic, split
    Soft butter

Rub with a garlic clove and lightly butter a 2-quart baking dish.

    2 cups (8 ounces) Cheddar cheese, grated   1 egg
    5 or 6 medium potatoes; peeled, sliced, and   2 cups milk
       covered with cold water to prevent their dis-
       coloring

Prepare the cheese and potatoes. In a mixing bowl, beat together the egg and milk.

At this point you may stop and continue later.

    Nutmeg
    Salt
    Fresh-ground pepper

Drain the potatoes and dry them with absorbent paper. In the baking dish, arrange a layer of potatoes, then a layer of the cheese. Season them with nutmeg, salt, and pepper. Repeat, finishing with a layer of potatoes. Pour the egg-milk over all.

    Bake the dish, uncovered, at 350° for 45 minutes, or until the top is golden and the liquid is absorbed.

Braised Lettuce

DOUBLES

PREPARATION: 10 MINUTES
COOKING: 10 MINUTES

    3 medium-large heads Boston lettuce

Trim the lettuce, if necessary; rinse it under cold running water, but do not pull it apart. Drain it well. Arrange the lettuce heads in a skillet with a lid.

⅓ cup water
3 tablespoons butter
1 vegetable bouillon cube

In a saucepan, combine the water, butter, and bouillon cube.

At this point you may stop and continue later.

Heat the water to dissolve the bouillon cube. Pour the liquid over the lettuce and simmer it, covered, for 5 minutes, or until it is tender.

Remove the lettuce to a serving dish; cut each head in half. Keep the lettuce warm while you reduce the pan juices over high heat. When the liquid is slightly thickened, pour over the lettuce and serve.

Indian Pudding

PREPARATION: 30 MINUTES
COOKING: 1 HOUR IN A 350° F. OVEN

If you prepare all of the ingredients in advance, making Indian Pudding —like soufflé—is a speedy, last minute operation. If desired, 1 cup of thin-sliced, peeled apple may be used to line the bottom of the dish before you add the cornmeal mixture.

1 quart milk, scalded
6 tablespoons cornmeal

In the top of a double boiler, combine the milk and cornmeal and, over boiling water, cook the mixture, stirring often, for 20 minutes.

2 tablespoons butter   ¼ teaspoon ginger
¾ cup light molasses   1 teaspoon salt
1 teaspoon cinnamon

Stir in these five ingredients.

At this point, you may stop and continue later. (If you have stopped, reheat the cornmeal mixture before continuing.)

2 eggs, lightly beaten

Away from the heat, beat in the eggs.

1 cup cold milk

Spoon the mixture into a lightly buttered baking dish. Over it, pour the cold milk.

Cream or vanilla ice cream (optional)

Bake the pudding, uncovered, at 350° for 1 hour, or until it is set (it will be of soft consistency). Serve it at once with cream or, if desired, vanilla ice cream.

Baked Stuffed Mushrooms
Eggplant and Zucchini in Custard
Broccoli with Lemon Butter, page 126
Carrots with Raisins
Pears with Chocolate Sauce, page 21

FOR 6 PERSONS

The pleasure of preparing ahead! (A refrain you hear often in this book.) The mushrooms may be totally readied for cooking. The eggplant and zucchini may be prepared up to the point of adding the custard and the final baking. The broccoli should be cooked as near as possible to the time of serving it, but the carrots may be fully cooked and briefly reheated. The pears and their sauce are readied well ahead of time.

Baked Stuffed Mushrooms

DOUBLES

PREPARATION: 25 MINUTES
COOKING: 30 MINUTES IN A 350° F. OVEN

A delightful dish which I first enjoyed at the home of friends in Rome, and from whom I coaxed the recipe.

24 large mushrooms, the stems removed and trimmed

Chop the mushroom stems fine and remove the caps.

1½ cups breadcrumbs	**½ teaspoon salt**
¼ cup fine-chopped parsley	**¼ teaspoon pepper**
1 clove garlic, peeled and	
pressed	

In a mixing bowl, combine the chopped mushroom stems, breadcrumbs, parsley, garlic, and salt and pepper. Toss the mixture to blend it well.

4 tablespoons butter, melted
⅓ cup hot water, in which 2 vegetable bouillon cubes are
dissolved
Reserved mushroom caps

Gradually add the butter and broth, tossing the crumbs to moisten them evenly. With this mixture, stuff the reserved mushroom caps, mounding the stuffing slightly at the center.

Arrange the mushrooms in an oven-proof serving dish, the cup side down.

At this point you may stop and continue later.

¾ cup dry white wine

Add the wine to the dish and bake the mushrooms, uncovered, at 350° for 30 minutes, basting them frequently with the wine.

Eggplant and Zucchini in Custard

DOUBLES (THOUGH IT IS REALLY EASIER TO MAKE 2)

PREPARATION: 45 MINUTES
COOKING: 40 MINUTES IN A 350° F. OVEN

An Italian dish first enjoyed when I was in Rome searching out inter-esting vegetable recipes.

Olive oil
1 large eggplant, unpeeled and cut into ¼-inch slices
4 medium zucchini, cut into ¼-inch slices

In olive oil, sauté the eggplant on both sides. Remove it to absorbent paper. Repeat the process with the zucchini.

½ cup fine-chopped parsley
1 teaspoon basil
Salt
Fresh-ground pepper

Cut the eggplant slices into quarters. In a lightly oiled oven-proof serving dish, arrange the eggplant in an even layer. Over it, sprinkle one-half of the parsley, basil, and salt and pepper to taste. Repeat with the zucchini.

4 medium tomatoes, peeled, seeded, and chopped
1 large onion, peeled and chopped fine

Over the top, spread evenly first the tomatoes and then the onion.

1 cup light cream or half-and-half
1 egg
½ teaspoon cinnamon
1 egg yolk (optional)

In a mixing bowl, beat together the cream, egg, and cinnamon. (If a firmer custard is desired, add 1 egg yolk.)

At this point, you may stop and continue later.

½ pound mozzarella cheese, thin sliced

Over the contents of the baking dish, pour the prepared custard mix-ture. Garnish the dish with mozzarella slices. Bake the loaf in the upper third of the oven at 350° for 40 minutes, or until the cheese is set.

Carrots with Raisins

DOUBLES / REFRIGERATES

PREPARATION: 15 MINUTES
COOKING: 12 MINUTES

If desired, the butter may be omitted.

5 tablespoons butter	Fresh-grated nutmeg
½ cup dry white wine	Salt
1 tablespoon sugar	Fresh-ground white pepper
6 large or 12 medium carrots, scraped and sliced thin	½ cup golden raisins, plumped for 5 minutes in hot water and drained

In a skillet with a lid or a large saucepan, melt the butter and to it add the wine and sugar. Add the carrots, stirring to coat them well. Cover them and, over high heat, cook them, shaking the pan occasionally, for 12 minutes, or until they are tender-crisp and the liquid is nearly absorbed. Season them and over them sprinkle the raisins.

Garlic Soup
Casserole of Barley and Mushrooms
Chopped Spinach
Mixed Green Salad, page 245
Chocolate-Orange Mousse

FOR 6 PERSONS

The flavor of garlic soup is delicate, not in the least overwhelming. The casserole has a fresh herbal taste. A light, healthful meal is given panache by the glamour of an unusual dessert.

Garlic Soup

DOUBLES / REFRIGERATES / FREEZES

PREPARATION: 1 HOUR

12 cloves garlic
4 tablespoons butter
¼ cup fine-chopped parsley

In a saucepan, put the garlic through a press. Add the butter and parsley and, over gentle heat, cook the mixture, stirring, for 5 minutes.

6 cups boiling water
6 vegetable bouillon cubes
1 medium potato, peeled
   and cubed fine

¼ teaspoon rosemary, crumbled
¼ teaspoon thyme
½ teaspoon pepper

Add these six ingredients and, over gentle heat, simmer the mixture, covered, for 45 minutes. In the container of an electric blender, whirl the mixture on medium speed, 2 cups at a time, for 15 seconds, or until it is smooth.

½ cup light cream, scalded
Grated Parmesan cheese

Add the cream to the soup. Over gentle heat, bring the soup to serving temperature. Adjust the seasoning to taste and garnish each serving with a sprinkling of the cheese.

Casserole of Barley and Mushrooms

DOUBLES / REFRIGERATES

PREPARATION: 20 MINUTES
COOKING: 50 MINUTES IN A 350° F. OVEN

If desired, 2 teaspoons of curry powder (or more, to taste) may be used in place of the herbs.

6 tablespoons butter
1 pound mushrooms, quartered
1 large onion, peeled and chopped

In a flame-proof casserole, heat the butter and in it cook the mushrooms and onion until the onion is translucent.

1½ cups medium pearl barley	½ teaspoon thyme
	1 teaspoon salt
½ teaspoon dill weed	½ teaspoon pepper
½ teaspoon marjoram	

Add the barley, stirring to coat each grain. Stir in the seasonings.

At this point you may stop and continue later.

3 cups boiling water, in which 3 vegetable bouillon cubes are dissolved

Add the bouillon and bake the casserole, covered, at 350° for 50 minutes, or until the barley is tender and the liquid is absorbed. Stir the dish occasionally as it cooks.

Chopped Spinach

Cook spinach as directed on page 69. Press it dry in a colander, chop it fine, and reheat it at the time of serving. Prepared in this way, spinach may be readied well ahead of time.

Chocolate-Orange Mousse

REFRIGERATES

PREPARATION: 45 MINUTES
CHILLING TIME: 6 HOURS

2 eggs
½ cup sugar

In a mixing bowl, beat the eggs and sugar together until satiny.

¼ cup water
One 6-ounce package semisweet chocolate bits
Grated rind of 1 orange
3 tablespoons orange-flavored liqueur

In the top of a double boiler, combine the water and chocolate bits. Over simmering water, dissolve the chocolate. Allow it to cool and add it to the egg mixture, together with the orange rind and liqueur.

Juice of 1 orange
2 teaspoons unflavored gelatin

Sieve the orange juice into a saucepan. Over it, sprinkle the gelatin. When the gelatin has softened, dissolve it over gentle heat. Add it to the chocolate mixture.

Chill the mixture until it has just begun to set.

1 cup heavy cream whipped

Into the chocolate mixture, fold the whipped cream. Spoon the mousse into a serving dish and chill it for at least 6 hours.

Cream of Turnip Soup
Fruit-filled Acorn Squash
Braised Cabbage, page 189
Prune Pie

FOR 6 PERSONS

Except for the cabbage, a somewhat unusual menu: few of us are acquainted with cream of turnip soup (I had never heard of it until I stumbled on it, happily, in the course of my experimentation); the apple and orange give the squash a new, light flavor; and the pie is made with sour cream and honey—a departure from more commonplace fruit pies.

Cream of Turnip Soup

DOUBLES / REFRIGERATES / FREEZES

PREPARATION: 45 MINUTES

> 1 pound white turnips,   1 medium onion, peeled and
>   peeled and sliced   sliced
> 1 medium potato, peeled   3 cups water
>   and sliced   4 vegetable bouillon cubes

In a large saucepan, combine these five ingredients. Bring the liquid to
the boil, reduce the heat, and simmer the vegetables, covered, for 30
minutes, or until they are very tender.

In the container of an electric blender, whirl the mixture, 2 cups at a
time, on medium speed for 15 seconds, or until it is smooth. Transfer
it to a second saucepan.

> ½ cup heavy cream, scalded
> ¼ cup fine-chopped parsley
> Salt
> Fresh-ground pepper

To the soup, add the cream, parsley, and salt and pepper to taste.

Fruit-Filled Acorn Squash

PREPARATION: 1¼ HOURS
COOKING: 30 MINUTES IN A 375° F. OVEN

> 3 acorn squash, halved

Arrange the squash on a baking sheet and bake them at 375° for 1 hour.

> 3 or 4 firm tart apples,   ½ cup dark brown sugar
>   peeled, cored, and diced   4 tablespoons butter, melted
> Juice of 1 lemon, sieved   ½ teaspoon salt
> 1 orange, peeled, seeded,
>   and chopped

Prepare the fruit: toss the apple with the lemon juice to prevent its
discoloring; add the remaining ingredients and toss the mixture to
blend it well.

At this point you may stop and continue later.

Remove the seeds from the squash. Fill the cavities with the fruit mixture. Bake the squash at 375° for 30 minutes, or until it is fork-tender.

Prune Pie

REFRIGERATES

PREPARATION: 15 MINUTES
COOKING: 45 MINUTES IN A 400° F. OVEN

One 9-inch pastry shell and top crust, page 237
Prepare the pastry.

2 cups (packed) cooked prunes, well drained, and chopped
Prepare the prunes and reserve them.

2 eggs	**Grated rind and juice of 1**
1 cup sour cream	**small lemon**
½ cup honey	**¼ teaspoon salt**

In a mixing bowl, combine these six ingredients and, with a rotary beater, blend them well. Add the prunes.

At this point you may stop and continue later.

Spoon the prune mixture into the pastry shell. Add the top crust, crimping the edges with the tines of a fork, and piercing the top to allow steam to escape.

Bake the pie at 400° for 45 minutes, or until it is golden brown. Serve hot or at room temperature.

Sweet Potato Soup
Turnip Ring
Collard Greens
Pears with Chocolate Sauce, page 21
Oatmeal Cookies, page 250

FOR 6 PERSONS

Two unusual dishes—sweet potato soup and turnip ring—and an un-usual vegetable "star" in this menu which culminates in the ever-pleasant flavor of pears. Excepting the soup, the meal is light; you may wish to add a cheese course. I do, and it seems to be appreciated.

Sweet Potato Soup

DOUBLES / REFRIGERATES / FREEZES

PREPARATION: 1 HOUR

In winter, serve the soup hot; in summer, offer it cold, as you would vichyssoise.

3 medium sweet potatoes, peeled and chopped coarse	2 ribs celery, chopped coarse
	3 cups water
	3 vegetable bouillon cubes
2 medium onions, peeled and chopped coarse	1 teaspoon tarragon
2 medium carrots, scraped and chopped coarse	

In a large saucepan or soup kettle, combine these seven ingredients. Bring the liquid to the boil, reduce the heat, and simmer the vegetables for 40 minutes, or until they are very tender.

In the container of an electric blender, whirl the contents of the saucepan, 2 cups at a time, on medium speed, for 15 seconds, or until the mixture is smooth. Transfer it to a second saucepan.

Milk
Salt
Fresh-ground white pepper

Add milk to the purée until the soup is the consistency of your choice. Season it to taste.

Chopped chives

Serve the soup garnished with chopped chives.

Turnip Ring

PREPARATION: 50 MINUTES
COOKING: 35 MINUTES IN A 375° F. OVEN

6 to 8 white turnips

In boiling salted water to cover, cook the turnips, covered, for 40 minutes, or until they are very tender. Drain, peel, and mash them until smooth. Measure 2 cups of the purée and reserve it.

2½ tablespoons butter	**1 tablespoon sugar**
3 tablespoons flour	**4 eggs yolks**
1 cup milk	**½ teaspoon ground cumin**

In a saucepan, heat the butter and in it, over gentle heat, cook the flour for a few minutes. Gradually add the milk, stirring constantly until the mixture is thickened and smooth. Beat in the sugar, egg yolks, and cumin.

Reserved turnip purée
Salt
Fresh-ground white pepper

Add the 2 cups of turnip purée and blend the mixture well. Season it to taste.

At this point you may stop and continue later.

4 egg whites, beaten until stiff but not dry
Fine-chopped parsley

Into the turnip mixture, fold the egg white. Spoon the batter into a lightly buttered 1½-quart ring mold. Bake the turnip ring at 375° for 35 minutes, or until it is set. Remove it from the oven, and allow it to rest for 5 minutes. Unmold it onto a warm serving platter and garnish it with parsley.

Collard Greens

REFRIGERATES

PREPARATION: 10 MINUTES
COOKING: 35 MINUTES

If you prefer, frozen chopped collard greens may be used. Follow the instructions on the package.

2 pounds fresh collard greens

Remove the woody stems from the collard greens and rinse the leaves thoroughly in cold water. Arrange them in a large saucepan or soup kettle with only the water that clings to the leaves.

Soft butter
Salt
Fresh-ground pepper

Place the kettle over high heat. When steam starts to rise, reduce the heat to low, cover the greens, and simmer them for 35 minutes, or until they are tender. Drain them (reserving the liquid for use in some other recipe), chop them coarse, and season them with butter, salt, and pepper to taste.

Raw Mushroom Soup
Hominy Ring
Braised Red Cabbage, page 121
Mixed Green Salad, page 245
Banana Tart

FOR 6 PERSONS

An unusual soup and an unusual main dish are highlighted in this menu. I suggest you serve the cabbage truly as a side dish—that is, in a plate by itself. The cool salad prepares the palate for the tasty banana tart.

Raw Mushroom Soup

DOUBLES / REFRIGERATES / FREEZES

PREPARATION: 25 MINUTES

A soup redolent with the flavor of mushrooms, quite different from the version found on page 162.

1 pound mushrooms, chopped coarse	½ teaspoon powdered cumin
2 cups milk	¼ teaspoon pepper
2 vegetable bouillon cubes, powdered	

In the container of an electric blender, combine these five ingredients and, on medium speed, whirl them for 15 seconds, or until the mixture is smooth. Transfer it to the top of a double boiler.

1 cup milk
1 cup sour cream
Salt

Add the milk and the sour cream, stirring to blend the soup well. Season it with salt to taste.

Chopped chives

Over boiling water, heat the soup until it is very hot and allow it to cook, covered, for 10 minutes. Garnish each serving with chopped chives.

Hominy Ring

REFRIGERATES

PREPARATION: 10 MINUTES IN A 375° F. OVEN

5 cups water	1 bunch scallions, trimmed
1½ teaspoons salt	and chopped fine, with
1¼ cups quick-cooking	the firm green part
hominy	⅓ cup fine-chopped parsley

Season the water with the salt; bring it rapidly to the boil and stir in the hominy. Reduce the heat to medium and cook the hominy, covered, for 30 minutes. Stir in the scallions and parsley.

Spoon the mixture into a lightly oiled 1½-quart ring mold and allow it to stand for 30 minutes. Unmold it.

1 egg
1 tablespoon melted butter

In a mixing bowl, beat together the egg and butter. Brush the hominy ring generously with this mixture.

¼ cup breadcrumbs
¼ cup grated Parmesan cheese

In a mixing bowl, combine the breadcrumbs and cheese. Generously dust the ring mold with this mixture. Replace the hominy ring in the mold.

At this point you may stop and continue later.

Tomato Sauce, page 253

Bake the ring mold at 375° for 10 minutes, or until it is golden. Unmold the ring and serve it with tomato sauce.

Banana Tart

PREPARATION: 35 MINUTES
CHILLING TIME: 3 HOURS

The preparation time does not include readying the pastry.

One 8-inch pastry shell, fully baked, page 237

Prepare the pastry.

4 large ripe bananas, peeled and the threads removed	½ cup sugar
	½ teaspoon nutmeg
	Pinch of salt
1 tablespoon butter	1 envelope unflavored gelatin

Sieve the bananas into a saucepan. Add the butter, sugar, nutmeg, and salt. Over medium heat, cook the mixture, stirring constantly, until it comes to the boil. Over it, sprinkle the gelatin and stir to dissolve it. Allow the mixture to cool.

Juice of 1 lime
Juice of 1 large orange

Stir in the lime and orange juice and chill.

1 cup heavy cream, whipped
Prepared pastry shell

When the banana mixture has just started to set, fold in the whipped cream. Spoon the filling into the pastry shell and refrigerate the tart for 3 hours, or until it is set.

Swedish Vegetable Soup
Squash Soufflé
Braised Fennel, page 198
Crêpes Suzette

FOR 4 PERSONS

While the soup derives from Sweden, the soufflé and fennel come from my kitchen, and the classic dessert from France—an international meal in which detente of flavors is the key note. Also, it is an easily prepared, do-ahead meal.

Swedish Vegetable Soup

DOUBLES / REFRIGERATES

PREPARATION: 25 MINUTES
COOKING: 30 MINUTES

6 tablespoons butter
4 medium carrots, scraped
　and sliced thin
1 medium cauliflower, sepa-
　rated into flowerets
3 leeks, well rinsed and
　chopped (or 1 bunch
　scallions)

2 large onions, peeled and
　sliced
4 medium potatoes, peeled
　and diced

In a soup kettle, heat the butter and in it cook the vegetables, stirring often to coat them well, until the butter is absorbed.

5 cups water
4 vegetable bouillon cubes
1 bay leaf
½ teaspoon basil

½ teaspoon marjoram
½ teaspoon savory
½ teaspoon thyme
4 peppercorns

Add the water and bouillon cubes. Add the herbs, tied together in cheesecloth. Bring the liquid to the boil, reduce the heat, and simmer the vegetables, covered, for 30 minutes, or until they are tender.

Salt
¼ cup fine-chopped parsley

Remove the cheesecloth bag. Season the soup with salt to taste. Garnish it with parsley.

Squash Soufflé

PREPARATION: 20 MINUTES
COOKING: 45 MINUTES IN A 350° F. OVEN

All ingredients for the soufflé, and its dish, may be readied ahead of time. The preparation time does not include readying the squash. The recipe works equally well if you use one 10-ounce package frozen mashed Hubbard squash, fully thawed to room temperature.

4 tablespoons butter   ¼ teaspoon nutmeg
4 tablespoons flour   1 teaspoon salt
¾ cup milk   ¼ teaspoon white pepper

In a saucepan, heat the butter and in it, over gentle heat, cook the flour, stirring, for a few minutes. Gradually add the milk, stirring constantly until the mixture is thickened and smooth. Stir in the seasonings.

1½ cups cooked, mashed winter squash

Stir in the squash.

4 egg yolks

Beat in the egg yolks.

4 egg whites, beaten until stiff but not dry

Into the squash mixture, fold the egg white. Spoon the mixture into a buttered 2-quart soufflé dish. Bake the soufflé at 350° for 45 minutes, or until it is well puffed and golden. Serve it at once.

Crepes Suzetté

Follow the directions for Crêpes, page 239, using the recipe for dessert crêpes. Reserve the cooked crêpes and prepare the following syrup:

3 tablespoons sugar	Juice of 1 lemon, sieved
Grated rind of 1 orange	6 tablespoons butter
Juice of 2 oranges, sieved	Few grains of salt

In a saucepan, combine these six ingredients. Cook them only until the sugar is dissolved and the butter melted.

At this point you may stop and continue later.

In a skillet or chafing dish (if you prepare the dessert at the table), heat the prepared syrup. In it, warm the crêpes and remove them to a serving dish (folding them in quarters makes them attractive). Over them, pour the remaining syrup.

¼ cup orange-flavored liqueur
¼ cup cognac
Confectioners' sugar

In a saucepan, combine the liqueur and cognac. Warm the liquid, ignite it, and pour it over the crêpes. When the flame dies, dust the crêpes with the sugar and serve them.

Baked Mushroom Canapés, page 31
Hominy Soufflé
Zucchini
Salad, page 245
Cheese, page 248
Fresh Fruit, page 248

FOR 6 PERSONS

What a pretty meal this is! The round mushrooms, the light-colored soufflé contrasting with the green zucchini, the fresh crispness of the salad, and the colors of the fruit. I suggest two cheeses: a blue and a Brie, served with plain Melba toast. And I suggest two fruits: red Delicious apples and Anjou pears, both chilled. A light, red wine will enhance the menu.

Hominy Soufflé

PREPARATION: 45 MINUTES
COOKING: 45 MINUTES IN A 375° OVEN

    1 cup water
    1 teaspoon salt
    ¾ cup quick-cooking hominy grits

Bring the water to the boil in the top of a double boiler. Add the salt and hominy and cook the mixture over direct heat, stirring, for 2 minutes.

    1 cup milk

Stir in the milk and, over simmering water, cook the hominy for 30 minutes.

1 cup warm milk
4 tablespoons soft butter
½ cup grated cheese of your choice

Add these three ingredients, stirring until the cheese is melted.

4 egg yolks
Salt
¼ teaspoon white pepper

Away from the heat, beat in the egg yolks. Season the batter.

4 egg whites, beaten stiff but not dry

Fold the egg white into the hominy mixture. Spoon the mixture into a buttered 2-quart soufflé dish and bake it at 375° for 45 minutes, or until the soufflé is well puffed and golden. Serve it at once.

Zucchini

DOUBLES / REFRIGERATES

PREPARATION: 10 MINUTES
COOKING: 10 MINUTES

3 tablespoons butter
6 medium zucchini,
    trimmed, cut into
    ½-inch slices, and
    rinsed in cold water

2 cloves garlic, peeled and
    put through a press
1 vegetable bouillon cube,
    powdered
Fresh-ground pepper

In a skillet, heat the butter. Add the zucchini with only the water that clings to them. Add the garlic, the bouillon powder, and a fresh grinding of pepper.

Over high heat, bring the contents of the skillet to the steaming point. Reduce the heat to low, cover the skillet, and simmer the zucchini in its own liquid, shaking the pan often, for 10 minutes, or until the vegetable is tender-crisp. Remove the lid and, over high heat, rapidly evaporate the liquid.

Artichokes, page 201
Onion and Olive Quiche
Salad, page 245
Dried-fruit Compote, page 193
Oatmeal Cookies, page 250

FOR 6 PERSONS

Serve the artichokes hot with either Lemon Butter, page 252, or heated Vinaigrette Sauce, page 254. With the quiche, offer a sumptuous salad composed of several different greens and vegetables tossed with Oil-and-Lemon Dressing, page 256. Include a cheese course, if you wish; the Parmesan in the quiche does not replace it. A dollop of sour cream on the fruit compote will glamorize it considerably!

Onion and Olive Quiche

PREPARATION: 20 MINUTES
COOKING: 30 MINUTES IN A 425°/325° F. OVEN

The preparation time does not include readying the pastry.

One 9-inch pastry shell, page 237

Prepare the pastry.

   3 tablespoons olive oil
   4 large onions, peeled and chopped
   Thyme

In a skillet, heat the oil and in it cook the onion, seasoned with a sprinkling of thyme, until it is translucent.

1 cup pitted ripe olives, drained and sliced

Prepare the olives.

3 eggs, lightly beaten	½ teaspoon salt
2 cups light cream	¼ teaspoon pepper
¼ cup grated Parmesan cheese	

In a mixing bowl, combine and blend these five ingredients.

At this point you may stop and continue later.

Dijon-style mustard

Using a pastry brush, delicately paint the pie shell with mustard. Over the bottom of the shell, arrange the onion in an even layer. Add the olives. Pour the custard over all.

Bake the quiche at 425° for 10 minutes; reduce the heat to 325° and continue baking it for 20 minutes, or until the custard is set and the crust is golden. Allow it to stand for 5 minutes before cutting it.

Cream of Carrot Soup, page 79
Potato Puff
Wilted Spinach, page 36
Pears with Chocolate Sauce, page 21

FOR 6 PERSONS

A meal with pleasing color accents—the faint orange of the soup contrasting with the golden potato puff, itself complemented by the deep green of the spinach, all climaxed by the delicate shade of the pears and the rich brown of their sauce. The contrasting flavors are pleasant, too!

Potato Puff

PREPARATION: 15 MINUTES
COOKING: 1 HOUR IN A 350° F. OVEN

1 cup milk	3 medium potatoes, peeled
3 egg yolks	and chopped coarse
1 medium onion, chopped	1½ teaspoon salt
coarse	¼ teaspoon pepper
1 cup grated Cheddar cheese	

In the container of an electric blender, combine these seven ingredients and, on medium speed, whirl them until the mixture is smooth. Transfer it to a mixing bowl.

⅓ cup fine-chopped parsley
1 small green pepper, seeded and diced fine

Stir in the parsley and pepper.

At this point you may stop and continue later.

3 egg whites, beaten until stiff but not dry

Fold the egg white into the potato mixture. Spoon the batter into a buttered 2-quart soufflé dish. Bake the potato puff at 350° for 1 hour, or until it is well risen and golden. Serve it at once.

Swedish Vegetable Soup, page 223
Artichoke Quiche
Curried Brussels Sprouts, page 135
Fresh Pineapple, page 181

FOR 6 PERSONS

A light and *"galant"* menu, delightful for an intimate supper party. Enliven the meal with a dry white wine served well chilled.

Artichoke Quiche

PREPARATION: 25 MINUTES
COOKING: 30 MINUTES IN A 425°/325° F. OVEN

The preparation time does not include readying the pastry.

One 9-inch pastry shell, page 237
Prepare the pastry.

Three 8-ounce packages frozen artichoke hearts
Following the directions on the package, cook the artichoke hearts until they are barely tender. Drain and refresh them in cold water. Drain them thoroughly on absorbent paper. Chop them coarse.

3 tablespoons butter
2 medium onions, peeled and chopped
In a skillet, heat the butter and in it cook the onions until translucent.

3 eggs, lightly beaten   **½ teaspoon salt**
2 cups light cream   **¼ teaspoon pepper**
½ cup grated Parmesan cheese
In a mixing bowl, combine and blend these five ingredients.

At this point you may stop and continue later.

Over the bottom of the pie shell, arrange in even layers, first the onion and then the artichokes. Over all, pour the custard.

Bake the quiche at 425° for 10 minutes; reduce the heat to 325° and continue baking it for 20 minutes, or until the custard is set and the crust is golden. Allow it to stand for 5 minutes before cutting it.

The Basics:
for All Seasons

Breads and Pastry

Muffins

DOUBLES / REFRIGERATES / FREEZES

MAKES 12 MUFFINS
PREPARATION: 10 MINUTES
COOKING: 12 MINUTES IN A 400° F. OVEN

Light, quick, and easy, muffins, made as directed here, are easily produced, hot and golden, and, when a bread is desired, are always welcome.

- 2 cups flour
- 3 teaspoons baking powder
- 2 tablespoons sugar
- ½ teaspoon salt

In a mixing bowl, sift together these dry ingredients.

- 1 egg
- 1 cup milk
- 4 tablespoons melted butter, slightly cooled

In a mixing bowl, using a rotary beater, blend well these liquid ingredients. Butter 12 muffin cups.

At this point you may stop and continue later.

To the dry ingredients, add the liquid, stirring only sufficiently to moisten the flour. Fill the prepared muffin cups two-thirds full. Bake the muffins at 400° for 12 minutes, or until they are well risen and lightly browned.

The following variants on the basic muffin recipe will provide pleasant changes:

Blueberry muffins: 1 cup blueberries, rinsed, drained, and tossed with ¼ cup of the suggested flour; increase the sugar to ½ cup.

Cheese muffins: to the liquid ingredients, add ½ cup grated cheese of your choice.

Cornmeal muffins: use ¾ cup cornmeal and 1½ cups flour; if desired, use ¼ cup maple syrup in place of the sugar.

Cranberry muffins: use 1 cup cranberries, rinsed, drained, chopped, and blend in ½ cup sugar.

Herb muffins: to the dry ingredients, add ½ teaspoon each: oregano, sage, and thyme.

Oatmeal muffins: use 1 cup quick-cooking oatmeal in place of 1 cup of the flour.

Roquefort (Blue Cheese) muffins: to the liquid ingredients, add ½ cup crumbled Roquefort or blue cheese.

Wheat Germ muffins: use 1 cup wheat germ in place of 1 cup of the flour; increase the baking powder to 4 teaspoons, the sugar to ⅓ cup, the milk to 1¼ cups, and the butter to 5 tablespoons; bake the muffins at 425° for 20 minutes.

Whole Wheat and Orange muffins: use whole wheat flour, ⅓ cup sugar, grated rind of 2 oranges, the juice of 2 oranges combined with milk to equal 1 cup, 2 eggs, and ½ teaspoon orange extract.

Yogurt muffins: use plain yogurt in place of the milk.

Cornbread

DOUBLES / REFRIGERATES / FREEZES

PREPARATION: 15 MINUTES
COOKING: 20 MINUTES IN A 425° F. OVEN

¾ cup corn meal	⅓ cup sugar
1 cup flour	¾ teaspoon salt
1 tablespoon baking powder	

In a mixing bowl, sift together these dry ingredients.

1 cup milk
3 tablespoons melted butter
1 egg

In a mixing bowl, using a rotary beater, blend these liquid ingredients.

To the dry ingredients, add the liquid mixture, stirring only to moisten the flour.

Spoon the batter into a buttered 8 × 8-inch baking dish. Bake the cornbread at 425° for 20 minutes, or until it is well risen and golden.

Cream Biscuits

MAKES 12 TO 18 BISCUITS
PREPARATION: 10 MINUTES
COOKING: 12 MINUTES IN A 400° F. OVEN

> 1½ cups flour
> 1 tablespoon baking powder
> 1 teaspoon salt

In a mixing bowl, sift together these three ingredients.

> 1 cup heavy cream

Have the cream at room temperature. Lightly butter a baking sheet.

At this point you may stop and continue later.

> Note: at this point, for added flavor, you may add the grated
> rind of 1 lemon, or of 1 orange; or 1 tablespoon very fine-
> chopped onion; or ¾ teaspoon ground cardamom, or
> coriander, or oregano, or thyme.

To the dry ingredients, add the cream, stirring the mixture with a fork only to moisten the flour.

Drop the batter by the spoonful onto the prepared baking sheet. (The biscuit yield will depend upon the size of the spoon you use—a teaspoon for delicate biscuits, a tablespoon for more robust ones.)

Bake the biscuits at 400° for 12 minutes, or until they are risen and golden.

Short Pastry for Quiches, Tarts, and Pastry Shells

MAKES TWO 9-INCH QUICHE OR TART SHELLS
PREPARATION: 10 MINUTES

The secret of success lies in working quickly and lightly and in handling the dough as little as possible.

> 2 cups all-purpose flour, sifted
> 1¼ teaspoons salt

In a mixing bowl, combine and blend the flour and salt.

½ cup vegetable shortening
½ cup butter

Using a pastry blender or fork, cut the shortening and butter into the flour until the mixture forms even "kernels" the size of peas.

½ cup ice water

By the tablespoon, sprinkle the ice water over the flour, stirring with a fork until sufficient water has been added to enable the dough to be patted lightly into a ball. (It is possible that all the water may not be needed.)

Wrap the dough in plastic and chill it for about 1 hour.

Roll it out, line the utensil with it, and proceed with the recipe as directed.

Any remaining pastry may be frozen for future use.

Farinaceous Foods

Seasoned Flour

MAKES ⅔ CUP

⅔ cup flour
1½ teaspoons salt
½ teaspoon pepper
½ teaspoon paprika (optional)

In a paper bag, combine the ingredients, shaking to blend them well. To the bag, add, a few at a time, pieces of the vegetables you wish to dredge; shake the bag vigorously to coat the vegetable pieces and remove them.

For dredging in seasoned flour, vegetables should not be wet; they should be only as moist as they are naturally.

Frequently, remaining seasoned flour may be used to make the sauce for the dish in question.

Crêpes

REFRIGERATES / FREEZES

ABOUT 18 CRÊPES

PREPARATION: 1 HOUR
STANDING TIME: 2 HOURS

1½ cups flour	¾ cup milk
½ teaspoon salt	¾ cup water
2 eggs	5 tablespoons butter, melted

In the container of an electric blender, combine the ingredients and, on medium speed, whirl them for 20 seconds, or until the mixture is completely blended and smooth. Allow the batter to stand for at least 2 hours before making the crêpes.

Soft butter

Heat a 5- or 6-inch skillet or crêpe pan and butter it lightly. Pour in sufficient batter barely to cover the bottom of the pan (about 3 table-spoonfuls); tilt the pan to spread the batter evenly. Cook the crêpes as you would pancakes, first one side and then the other, turning them with a spatula. To refrigerate or freeze crêpes, put a piece of wax paper between each to prevent their sticking together and wrap them in plastic wrap.

For Dessert Crêpes: to the listed ingredients, add ¼ cup powdered sugar and 1 teaspoon vanilla or 3 tablespoons cognac or orange-flavored liqueur.

RICE AND BULGUR

Rice and bulgur (bulghur), among the most healthful and least fattening of starchy foods, are interchangeable in these menus. They are cooked in the same ways; they lend themselves to the same variations in seasonings; they add substance to a meal but do not make the diner feel heavy.

Two kinds of rice are readily available (wild rice, a member of the wheat family, is indeed *not* rice): white or polished rice is the most used; brown rice, free of its hull but unpolished, is enjoying increased popularity. It takes longer to cook than white rice but has more taste (a pleasantly nutty flavor) and, if frozen, retains its consistency better. Of the white varieties, there are long-grained, short-grained, Italian, Middle Eastern, and domestic, each with its own characteristics. I avoid precooked rice, finding natural rice more flavorful and of more pleasing consistency.

Bulgur (cracked wheat—available at specialty food stores) was originally a Middle Eastern food, popular also in Russia and eastern European countries. More flavorful than either white or brown rice, it is also best suited to freezing.

(One word about refrigerating and freezing rice or bulgur: before reheating to serve, the grain must be allowed to reach room temperature, and reheating must be done over gentle heat; heating cold, cooked grains over high heat results in overcooked mush. Use a fork to stir the grain.)

Boiled Rice or Bulgur

SERVES 6

DOUBLES / REFRIGERATES / FREEZES

PREPARATION: 10 MINUTES

COOKING: 20 MINUTES FOR WHITE RICE AND BULGUR;
          45 MINUTES FOR BROWN RICE

1½ tablespoons butter
1 small onion, chopped fine (optional)
1½ cups rice or bulgur

In a saucepan, heat the butter and in it cook the onion, if desired, until it is translucent. Add the grain, stirring to coat it well.

3 cups water, in which 3 vegetable bouillon cubes are
    dissolved

Prepare the water.

At this point you may stop and continue later.

Add the bouillon to the grain. Over high heat, bring the liquid to the boil; stir the grain once. Reduce the heat and simmer the grain, covered, for the length of time suggested above, or until it is tender and the liquid is absorbed.

The flavor of rice and bulgur is enhanced by various seasonings. After stirring the grain into the butter and onion mixture, but before the addition of the liquid, you may add any of the following seasonings:

1 teaspoon ground allspice
¾ teaspoon dried basil
1 bay leaf, broken
¾ teaspoon dried chervil
1 or 1½ teaspoons curry powder
¾ teaspoon dried dill weed
¾ teaspoon dried marjoram
1 or 1½ teaspoons dried mustard
Grated rind of 1 small orange
½ teaspoon dried rosemary, crumbled
¼ teaspoon saffron, crumbled
½ teaspoon dried sage, crumbled
½ teaspoon thyme

The cooking liquid may also be varied: you may use plain water seasoned with salt to taste (about 1 teaspoon), or home-made vegetable stock, or sieved fresh orange juice, or a combination of tomato juice and water (about half and half).

Rice or Bulgur en Casserole

Follow the recipe for Boiled Rice or Bulgur (page 240), using a flame-proof casserole in place of the saucepan. Bring the liquid to the boil before adding it to the grain; stir it once. Bake the grain, covered, at 350° F. for 18 to 25 minutes (white rice and bulgur) or 45 to 50 minused (brown rice).

NEW POTATOES

Rich in vitamins and minerals and less starchy than mature ones, new potatoes may be cooked in several ways. When the main dish of a given menu is made of potatoes, the recipe is included with the specific menu; these ideas are some you may want to try as side dishes.

Boiled New Potatoes

Scrub small new potatoes, allowing 2 or 3 per person; do not peel them. In a large saucepan, combine the potatoes, cold water to cover, and a generous sprinkling of salt. Bring the water to the boil and cook the potatoes, covered, for 10 to 15 minutes, or until they are just fork-tender. Drain and peel them, if you wish (I do not); add to them the garnishes of your choice (see below).

Steamed New Potatoes

Prepare the potatoes for cooking as suggested above. Arrange them in a vegetable steamer and, over rapidly boiling water, cook them, tightly covered, for 15 to 20 minutes, or until they are just fork-tender.

New potatoes may be garnished with one or a combination of the following:

Soft butter
Caraway seeds
Grated cheese of your choice
Dill weed, fresh or dried
Lemon, the grated rind or juice
Parsley, chopped
Pepper, fresh-ground
Scallions, chopped, with as much firm green as possible

Soups

The soups suggested in these menus are capable of many variations. For example, those recipes calling for flour as a thickening agent may be made instead with 1 medium potato, peeled, diced, and cooked with the other ingredients until very tender; the mixture then whirled in the container of an electric blender and the remainder of the recipe followed as directed. If a slightly sweet flavor is desired, use 1 medium sweet potato, peeled and diced.

Certain vegetables, cooked with the other ingredients of a given recipe, enhance the flavor of soup:

    1 medium carrot, scraped and diced
    Garlic, peeled and chopped fine, to taste (but use it carefully, as most soups are delicately flavored)
    1 or 2 leeks, thoroughly rinsed and chopped (in place of onion)
    1 medium onion, peeled and chopped (if desired, cooked in 2 tablespoons butter until translucent)
    1 medium parsnip, scraped and diced (for natural sweetness)
    1 or 2 white turnips, scraped and diced
    1 cup peeled and diced winter squash (acorn or butternut)

To give soup extra flavor and a visual accent, choose one of the following garnishes, added sparingly, to taste:

Cabbage, shredded fine
Celery, diced
Celery root (celeriac), peeled, cut in julienne strips, and blanched
Chives, chopped fine
Cucumber, peeled, seeded, and diced fine
Lettuce, shredded fine
Parsley, chopped fine
Peas, fresh or frozen, cooked
Radish, sliced thin
Rice, cooked
Spinach, the stems removed, shredded fine
Summer squash (yellow, zucchini), unpeeled and sliced thin
Tomato, peeled, seeded, and chopped

Garnishes

FOR VEGETABLE SIDE DISHES

In addition to enhancing your side dishes by never overcooking them and by presenting them in either attractive cook-and-serve ware or other appealing serving utensils, there are several garnishes which, used judiciously, add decoration and flavor. For cooks desiring side dishes which are simple rather than rich, I suggest:

Capers
Chives, chopped fine
Lemon (both the grated rind and the juice complement
   green vegetables)
Lime (use as you would lemon)
Mushrooms, sliced thin
Olives (green or ripe), chopped fine
Onion, chopped fine
Orange (use as you would lemon), for root vegetables
Parsley, chopped fine
Pepper (green or sweet red), seeded and chopped fine
Radish, sliced thin
Scallions, sliced thin
Tomato, peeled, seeded, and chopped
Watercress, chopped fine
Water chestnuts, sliced thin

For cooks unconcerned with calories:

Breadcrumbs (toasted in butter and sprinkled over the vegetable)
Brown butter (cook it over gentle heat until it is a rich golden color)
Cream, heavy (a little poured over the vegetable)
Cream, sour (served as a sauce at room temperature)
Croutons (toasted in butter and flavored, if desired, with an herb
   of your choice or garlic)

In addition, vegetables are given added taste and subtlety when cooked or sprinkled lightly with herbs or spices. Experimenting in this line is the best way to develop your own style and taste-signature. Among the many seasonings I use, both from my herb garden and the supermarket's spice shelf, the following are especially reliable:

Bay leaf (boil the bay leaf to flavor the water in which you cook
   the vegetable)
Celery seed or celery salt (sprinkle it over the cooked vegetable)
Cumin seed, ground (add it to the vegetable when cooking)
Curry powder (add it to the vegetable when cooking)
Dill (sprinkle it over the cooked vegetable)
Ginger (add it to root vegetables when cooking)
Marjoram (add it to the vegetable when cooking or sprinkle fresh
   over the prepared vegetable)

Mint (add it to the vegetable when cooking or sprinkle it, fresh-chopped, over the prepared vegetable)

Oregano (add it to the vegetable when cooking or sprinkle it over the prepared vegetable)

Poppy seed (sprinkle it over the cooked vegetable)

Rosemary (add it to the vegetable when cooking)

Sage (add it to the vegetable when cooking)

Sesame seed (sprinkle it over the cooked vegetable)

Summer Savoury (add it to the vegetable when cooking or sprinkle it, fresh-chopped, over the prepared vegetable)

Tarragon (add it to the vegetable when cooking or sprinkle it, fresh-chopped, over the prepared vegetable)

Thyme (add it to the vegetable when cooking)

See also the section in this chapter on Sauces and Dressings, page 251.

FOR DESSERTS

Crumb Topping for Fruit Tarts

PREPARATION: 10 MINUTES

4 tablespoons butter	¼ teaspoon cinnamon
½ cup dark brown sugar, packed	¼ teaspoon nutmeg
½ cup flour	Few grains of salt

In a saucepan, melt the butter and, away from the heat, add the brown sugar, flour, and seasonings. Using a fork, blend the mixture until it forms large crumbs.

Salads

MIXED GREEN SALAD

Salads should be tossed with their dressing only at the time of serving them. The greens and dressing may, however, be prepared ahead. Readied salad greens and accompanying vegetables may be refrigerated in plastic bags. Greens may be stored together, but their accompaniments (cucumber, scallions, tomatoes, etc.) should be kept separate so that each component of the salad retains its own individuality of flavor.

The following greens, tasty and visually attractive, may be used in almost any combination:

Arugola (also called rugola or roquette or rocket)
Celery cabbage
Endive
Escarole
Lettuce (all varieties)
Spinach
Watercress

One or more of the following vegetables may be added as a flavor or texture accent:

Artichoke hearts, cooked and chilled
Bamboo shoots
Broccoli stalk, raw, peeled, and cut into julienne strips
Carrot, grated
Celery, diced
Cherry tomatoes, whole or halved
Cucumber, sliced
Mushrooms, sliced
Hearts of palm
Green or red sweet pepper, cut into julienne strips
Radishes, sliced
Red onion, chopped or cut into rings
Scallions, chopped or cut lengthwise into 2-inch strips
Tomato wedges
Water chestnuts, sliced

If fresh herbs are available, give your salad added interest by sprinkling over the greens one or two of the following, cut fine with scissors:

Basil
Chervil
Chives
Dill weed
Marjoram
Oregano

Parsley
Summer Savory
Tarragon

Dried herbs will also enhance salad. Use them more sparingly than fresh herbs; their flavor is more concentrated.

You may embellish your salad by the addition of croutons (for texture) or of mimosa egg (sieved hard-boiled egg).

Mixed green salad, the most familiar of all salads, has no rule of thumb for its preparation. Its success depends upon experimenting with different combinations of greens until you find favorites of your own.

To prepare: Select a combination of greens which appeals to you. Rinse and dry them well; if you have no salad drier, swinging them in a large muslin towel is effective. Tear them into pieces of uniform size (sometimes I cut them with scissors—heresy, I know) and refrigerate them, as suggested above, until you are ready to toss them with your choice of dressings, pages 256–257.

Mixed Salad

SERVES 6

REFRIGERATES

PREPARATION: 15 MINUTES

1 large head Boston lettuce
Leaf lettuce of your choice (optional)

Wash and dry the greens. Tear them into pieces of your desired size. Arrange them in a salad bowl.

2 stalks celery, trimmed and diced
1 small cucumber, peeled and sliced
3 to 4 scallions, trimmed and cut in
   ½-inch rounds (or 1 medium
   red onion, peeled and sliced,
   the rings separated)

1 or 2 large ripe
   tomatoes, peeled
   and cut in wedges
Herb of your choice

Over the lettuce, arrange the remaining ingredients in an attractive pattern (assuming you are tossing the salad at the table). Add a sprinkling of fresh or dried herb of your choice, page 246.

Salad Dressing of your choice, pages 254, 256
Plain or flavored croutons (optional)

To the salad, after dressing it, you may add, if desired, plain or flavored croutons.

Desserts

ASSORTED CHEESE AND FRESH FRUIT

Although the majority of menus suggest "made" desserts, it is not *de rigueur* that you offer them. The desserts happen to go well, I feel, with the dishes preceding them; most of them are of the make-ahead, don't-worry variety. Though most are light, some are rich, so that, if you prefer a "leaner" dish—and I admit that I do, offering desserts rather infrequently—you may present your family and guests assorted cheese and fresh fruits in season.

Virtually every cheese goes well with fruit. I recommend hard or semi-soft cheeses, merely because they are more tidily eaten. Offer dry biscuits to accompany the cheese; almost any variety will serve your need. I have found the following cheeses to be especially complementary with fresh fruit; they are generally available at cheese shops, delicatessens, or supermarkets:

Appenzeller (Switzerland), tastes like "Swiss" cheese
Baronet (United States), mild and buttery
Bel Paese (Italy), soft and mild
"Blue" cheese (United States, Denmark), less elegant than the
  Roquefort of France, but very good
Brick (United States), a Cheddar-related cheese
Brie (France), perhaps the supreme soft-ripening cheese
Caerphilly (Wales), hard, tasting somewhat like buttermilk
Camembert (France), a near-relative of Brie (above)
Cantal (France), sometimes called "the French Cheddar"
Cheddar (England, United States, Canada), perhaps our most
  widely used cheese, also locally called "store cheese"

Edam (Holland), one of the world's best-known cheeses, mild and
semi-hard
Emmenthaler (Switzerland), the original and only genuine "Swiss"
cheese
Feta (Greece), a somewhat salty accompaniment to sweet fruit
Fontina (Italy), sweet, delicate-tasting
Gorgonzola (Italy), the supreme Italian blue cheese, poorly imi-
tated in this country
Gouda (Holland), rather similar to Edam (above), a fine table
cheese
Gruyère (Switzerland, France), similar to Emmenthaler (above)
but perhaps more flavorful
Jarlsberg (Norway), the bland Norwegian "Swiss"
Liederkranz (United States), one of the two cheeses native to this
country (the other is Brick); soft-ripening, pungent to the nose,
mild to the taste, excellent with apples
Livarot (France), semi-hard, zesty, its flavor milder than its scent
Monterey Jack (United States), together with Brick and Colby,
a Cheddar-related cheese
Münster (Alsace), semi-hard and pungent
Neufchâtel (Switzerland, United States), soft, white, bland, similar
to "cream cheese," excellent with strawberries
Parmesan (Italy), properly called Parmigiano-Reggiano, hard, pun-
gent, granular, excellent with all fruits
Pont l'Évêque (France), semi-hard, fairly strong-flavored
Port du Salut (France), originally a Trappist cheese; firm, fairly
mild
Ricotta (Italy, United States), a fresh cheese not imported from
Italy; the domestic product, less flavorful than the Italian, is a
nice accompaniment to berries
Roquefort (France), the supreme blue cheese, should be well-
veined and creamy with a pungent but not sharp taste
Stilton (England), the major English blue cheese, similar to but
milder than Roquefort
Tilsiter (Germany), also made in other countries; of medium-sharp
flavor

As for the fruit to accompany your choice of cheese, select those in
season and purchase them sufficiently in advance of using them so that
they will ripen well (the United States fruit-growing industry usually

ships its produce before it is ripe; it is left to the consumer to bring it *au point* for eating). To serve with cheese, I recommend:

Apples (Cortland, Delicious, Granny Smith—a new and excellent apple from South Africa—McIntosh, Winesap)
Apricots (*very* difficult to find fresh and ripe, but excellent with soft-ripening and cream cheeses)
Berries (blue-; black-; raspberries; and strawberries)
Cherries
Figs (if you can find ripe ones)
Grapes
Mangoes
Melons (with mild cheese)
Papayas
Peaches and nectarines
Pears (Bartlett, Comice, Bosc, Anjou)
Plums

In addition, fresh fruit compote is enhanced by cheese. If you wish to offer cooked dried-fruit compote, you will find cheese a pleasant addition to it. Guava shells, available canned, and quince, occasionally available at a fruiterer's and which must be cooked to be edible, are both excellent with soft, creamy cheeses.

Oatmeal Cookies

MAKES 36 COOKIES
FREEZES FOR STORAGE

PREPARATION: 30 MINUTES
COOKING: 15 MINUTES IN A 350° F. OVEN

Certainly oatmeal cookies are not elegant, but, well made, they are tasty, healthful, and fit happily into the frame of these vegetable menus.

8 tablespoons soft sweet butter
1 cup sugar
1 egg, beaten with ⅓ cup milk

In a mixing bowl, cream together the butter and sugar. Stir in the egg-milk mixture.

1¾ cups quick-cooking   ½ teaspoon allspice
    oatmeal   ¾ teaspoon cinnamon
1½ cups flour   ½ teaspoon cloves
½ teaspoon baking soda   ⅔ cup raisins
½ teaspoon salt

In a second mixing bowl, combine and blend thoroughly the oatmeal, flour, and seasonings. Stir in the raisins.

Combine the liquid and dry ingredients. Beat the batter briefly.

Drop the batter, one tablespoonful at a time, onto a buttered cookie sheet. Bake the cookies at 350° for 15 minutes, or until they are firm and their edges are slightly browned. Allow them to cool before storing them.

Sauces and Dressings

Aioli Sauce or Garlic Mayonnaise

A traditional French sauce from the region of Provence, aioli, *in former times, was made by the man of the family, usually in a large marble mortar which served both to grind the garlic and to whip the egg and oil. It was served over various vegetables dishes.*

To convert mayonnaise to *aioli,* simply add 1 or 2 cloves coarse-chopped garlic, to taste, to the 5 initial ingredients of the Mayonnaise recipe on pages 252–253.

Basil Sauce

MAKES ABOUT 1½ CUPS
DOUBLES / REFRIGERATES / FREEZES

PREPARATION: 10 MINUTES
"WORKING" TIME FOR SAUCE: 2 HOURS

A delicious sauce, simply made, for soufflés and main-dish puddings; it tastes best when served at room temperature.

1 cup mayonnaise
⅓ cup light cream
⅓ cup (packed) fresh basil leaves (dried basil will not do)

In the container of an electric blender, combine the three ingredients and, on medium speed, whirl them for 15 seconds, or until the mixture is smooth and the basil thoroughly chopped. Allow the sauce to "work" for at least 2 hours before using it.

Hollandaise Sauce

MAKES ABOUT 1¼ CUPS
PREPARATION: 15 MINUTES

4 egg yolks
2 tablespoons lemon juice
¼ teaspoon salt
Pinch of Cayenne

In the container of an electric blender, combine these four ingredients.

½ pound butter, melted and brought to the boil

Turn on the blender at medium speed. Into the contents of the container, pour the bubbling butter in a steady stream. Turn off the blender when the butter is used. Keep the Hollandaise warm by putting the container in hot water. It may be reblended if necessary.

For 4 persons: reduce the butter to ¼ pound, the egg yolks to 3.

Lemon Butter

In a small saucepan, melt 4 tablespoons butter or more, as desired; using a small whisk, whip into the butter the juice of ½ lemon or more, to taste, and a pinch of salt and white pepper. Pour the lemon butter over the vegetables.

Mayonnaise

MAKES ABOUT 1¼ CUPS
DOUBLES / REFRIGERATES

PREPARATION: 10 MINUTES

So much better when home-made, and so easily done in the container of an electric blender.

1 egg
¼ cup very light olive oil
　　or vegetable oil
2 teaspoons cider vinegar or
　　3 tablespoons lemon juice

½ to ¾ teaspoons dry
　　mustard
½ teaspoon salt

In the container of an electric blender, combine these five ingredients and, on medium speed, whirl them for a few seconds.

¾ cup oil

Without stopping the blender, add in a thin but steady stream the second quantity of oil. As soon as it is absorbed, shut off the blender.

Using a rubber spatula, transfer the mayonnaise to a jar with a tight-fitting lid and refrigerate it.

For Curried Mayonnaise, stir curry powder, to taste, into prepared mayonnaise; a suggested amount of curry for this recipe: 1 teaspoon. Add more for a more piquant dressing.

Piquant Sauce

MAKES ABOUT 1¼ CUPS
DOUBLES / REFRIGERATES

PREPARATION: 10 MINUTES

1 cup sour cream
1 clove garlic
1 teaspoon Dijon mustard
2 tablespoons prepared
　　horseradish

2 tablespoons cider vinegar
Salt
Fresh-ground pepper

In the container of an electric blender, combine the first five ingredients and, on medium speed, whirl them for 15 seconds, or until the mixture is smooth. Adjust the seasoning with salt and pepper to taste.

Tomato Sauce

MAKES ABOUT 3 CUPS

PREPARATION: 25 MINUTES

One 29-ounce can Italian tomatoes
1 large onion, peeled and chopped coarse

In the container of an electric blender, whirl the tomatoes, their liquid, and the onion, until they are reduced to a thin purée. Pour the purée into a skillet.

2 bay leaves	1 teaspoon salt
½ teaspoon oregano	¼ teaspoon pepper
2 teaspoons sugar	

Add the seasonings and simmer the tomatoes, uncovered, for 20 minutes, or until the sauce begins to thicken. Remove the bay leaves.

Vinaigrette Sauce

1 teaspoon salt	2 tablespoons water
1 teaspoon sugar	4 tablespoons vinegar of
½ teaspoon white pepper	your choice
1 teaspoon Dijon-style mustard	

In a jar with a tight-fitting lid, combine and shake these ingredients until the salt and sugar are dissolved.

¾ cup best grade olive oil

Add the olive oil to the contents of the jar and shake the mixture until it is thoroughly blended.

WHITE SAUCES

One recalls from one's childhood, or at least I do, an anemic mixture of butter, flour, and milk. It was often called "cream sauce," albeit cream never came near it; it resembled library paste in both appearance and texture. This noxious concoction, however, was—and is—capable of several sophisticated variations of flavor and consistency and, moreover, is an important element in many vegetable dishes.

Usually called Béchamel sauce (after a steward to Louis XIV), it is generally assumed to be of French origin (surely the simplest member of the lengthy canon of French sauces). Its genesis is also claimed by the Greeks, who had a thriving colony in the area which is now Marseilles. No matter; regardless of who invented this basic white sauce, it continues to be eminently useful.

There are four grades of Béchamel; save for the quantity of milk added to the *roux*, they are all made alike. The amount of liquid used determines their consistency, and hence their function. The four grades of Béchamel are:

1) a thin pouring sauce, often the basis of cream soups;
2) a thick pouring sauce, often used to dress vegetables;
3) a coating sauce, used to cover vegetables;
4) the *panada*, the basis of a 4-egg soufflé.

The cooking technique, the same for all four:

1) in a saucepan, melt the butter;
2) add the flour and, over gentle heat, cook the mixture (*roux*), stirring, for a few minutes;
3) gradually add the milk, salt (or a powdered vegetable bouillon cube), white pepper, and a grating of nutmeg to taste, stirring constantly until the mixture is thickened and smooth.

The quantities are:

1) for a thin pouring sauce:
   2 tablespoons butter
   2 tablespoons flour
   3 cups milk
2) for a thick pouring sauce:
   2 tablespoons butter
   2 tablespoons flour
   2 cups milk
3) for a coating sauce:
   2 tablespoons butter
   2 tablespoons flour
   1 or 1¼ cups milk
4) for a *panada*:
   4 tablespoons butter
   4 tablespoons flour
   1 cup milk

There are several variants possible with Béchamel sauce, all of them easy, all of them pleasant. Perhaps the most famous and most useful of the following eight sauces is Mornay (named for a sixteenth-century French statesman and Huguenot leader); but you will enjoy the possibilities afforded by using other ingredients and seasonings as well. It is for this reason that I include them; they will bring variation to your menu-making. To each cup of Béchamel sauce, add the suggested ingredients for the sauce of your choice:

AURORE: 2 tablespoons tomato purée and 1 tablespoon butter.

CHEESE: ½ cup grated Cheddar cheese and a little Worcestershire sauce, to taste.

DILL: 1 teaspoon dried dill weed (or more, to taste) or fresh-snipped dill and a little lemon juice, to taste.

HORSERADISH: 3 tablespoons (or to taste) drained prepared horseradish.

MORNAY: 2 tablespoons grated Swiss cheese, 2 tablespoons grated Parmesan cheese, 2 tablespoons butter. For Rich Mornay Sauce, add 1 egg yolk, beaten, and ¼ cup heavy cream.

MUSTARD: 1 tablespoon Dijon-style mustard or 1 teaspoon dried mustard.

PARSLEY AND LEMON: ¼ cup fine-chopped parsley, a grating of lemon rind, and a little lemon juice, to taste.

SOUBISE (named for Charles, Prince de Soubise, marshall of France in the eighteenth century): ½ cup fine-chopped onion, cooked until translucent in 2 tablespoons butter.

SALAD DRESSINGS

Blue Cheese Dressing

MAKES ABOUT 2 CUPS

REFRIGERATES

PREPARATION: 10 MINUTES

1 cup (4 ounces) crumbled blue cheese	Juice of 1 small lemon
	Salt
1 cup sour cream (or yogurt)	Pepper

In the container of an electric blender, whirl on medium speed the blue cheese, sour cream, and lemon juice for 15 seconds, or until the mixture is smooth. Season it to taste.

Oil-and-Lemon Dressing

MAKES ABOUT ⅔ CUP

PREPARATION: 5 MINUTES

Juice of 2 medium lemons	½ teaspoon salt
½ teaspoon sugar	¼ teaspoon white pepper
½ teaspoon dry mustard	½ cup mild olive oil

In a jar with a tight-fitting lid, combine the lemon juice and seasonings; shake the jar vigorously to dissolve the sugar and salt. Add the oil and shake the dressing once again.

Sesame Dressing

MAKES ABOUT 2 CUPS
REFRIGERATES

PREPARATION: 10 MINUTES

This recipe is a contribution of the artist Charles Blum, a country neighbor and a highly original cook.
The dressing keeps well in the refrigerator. Use it at room temperature on well-chilled greens.

1 cup vegetable oil (soy oil, preferably)
2 tablespoons refined sesame seed oil (available at specialty food shops)
⅓ cup lemon juice or rice vinegar
3 tablespoons soy sauce
1 teaspoon *tahine* (sesame seed purée, available at specialty food shops)
1 small onion, peeled and chopped coarse
1 clove garlic, peeled and chopped coarse
1 teaspoon sugar
Salt

In the container of an electric blender, combine all the ingredients except the salt. On medium speed, whirl them for 15 seconds, or until the mixture is homogenized. Adjust the seasoning.

Soy Dressing

MAKES ABOUT 1 CUP
DOUBLES / REFRIGERATES

PREPARATION: 10 MINUTES

For asparagus salad and for salads made with flavorful greens (arugola, watercress, etc.).

½ cup soy sauce
1½ tablespoons sugar
¼ teaspoon ginger

In a jar with a tight-fitting lid, combine these three ingredients. Shake them to dissolve the sugar.

2 tablespoons refined sesame seed oil

Add the oil and shake the dressing vigorously to blend it well.

DESSERT SAUCES

Brandy-and-Honey Sauce

MAKES ABOUT 1½ CUPS
REFRIGERATES

For fruit compotes and berries.

⅔ cup cognac
¼ cup fresh lemon juice, sieved
¾ teaspoon ginger
⅔ cup honey

In a jar with a tight-fitting lid, combine the ingredients and shake vigorously to blend them well.

Custard Sauce

MAKES ABOUT 2¼ CUPS
PREPARATION: 10 MINUTES

3 egg yolks, or 1 egg and 1 yolk, lightly beaten
¼ cup sugar
2 cups milk, scalded

In the top of a double boiler, combine the ingredients and, over simmering water, cook the mixture, stirring constantly, until the custard coats the spoon.

½ teaspoon vanilla or sweet sherry, to taste

Allow the custard to cool; stir in the flavoring of your choice and chill the sauce.

For a more sophisticated sauce: substitute ½ cup white port wine for an equal amount of the milk; in place of the vanilla or sherry, flavor the sauce with the grated rind of ½ lemon.

Lemon-Brandy Sauce

MAKES ABOUT 1½ CUPS
PREPARATION: 10 MINUTES

½ cup sugar
1 tablespoon cornstarch
1 cup water
2 tablespoons butter

Grated rind and juice of
1 lemon
Pinch of salt
¼ cup cognac

In a saucepan, combine the sugar and cornstarch, stirring to blend the mixture well. Add the water and cook the sauce, stirring constantly, until it is thickened and smooth. Add the remaining ingredients, stirring until the butter is melted. Allow the sauce to cool before chilling it.

Raspberry Sauce

MAKES 1¼ CUPS
DOUBLES / REFRIGERATES

PREPARATION: 15 MINUTES

One 10-ounce package frozen
  raspberries, fully thawed
  to room temperature

1 teaspoon cornstarch
Few grains of salt
Sugar

Into a saucepan, sieve the raspberries. Mix the cornstarch with a little of the berry juice; add it to the contents of the saucepan and cook the mixture, stirring, until it is thickened and smooth. Season the sauce to taste.

Poaching Syrup for Fruit Compotes

¾ cup sugar
1 cup water
Zest and juice of 1
  medium lemon
Zest and juice of
  1 orange

¼ cup grenadine syrup
  (optional)
4 allspice berries
One 3-inch piece cinnamon
  stick
4 whole cloves

In a saucepan, combine these ten ingredients, bring them to a rolling boil, and cook them for 5 minutes.

Add the prepared fruit and simmer it, uncovered, for 20 minutes, or until it is tender but still retains its shape. Remove the fruit to a serving dish with a slotted spoon. Strain the syrup over it. Allow the compote to cool before chilling it.

Menu-Making Index

The dishes listed alphabetically according to their menu category (appetizer, soup, main dish, side dish, salad, bread, and dessert), to facilitate the making of menus of the reader's choice.

MAIN DISHES

General Index

Robert Ackart

Robert Ackart has had three careers, first as a teacher of college English, then as an operatic stage director in Europe and America, and now as the author of five books on food and cooking. He evolves and tests recipes at his home in Katonah, New York, where, in season, he is an avid gardener and grows many of the foods he writes about in A Celebration of Vegetables. When not busy in the garden or the kitchen, Mr. Ackart enjoys sailing, music, and the travel that supplies many ideas for his books.